7-FIGURE
BUSINESS
OWNER

EFFIE HWANDE

ISBN: 979-8-218-32441-4

This publication is designed to provide accurate and authoritative information regarding the subject matter covered. It is sold with the understanding that the publisher is not engaged in rendering financial, accounting, or other professional advice. If financial advice or other expert assistance is required, the services of competent professional should be sought.

Printed in the United States of America

For information about training, contact Effie Hwande at **effiemedia.com**

Cover Design: Noel Hwande and Callie Revell
Interior Design: Callie Revell
Editor: Sandra Walters

Entrepreneurship is the bloodline of business, globally. As mandated and directed in Genesis 1:28, my belief is that we all have it in us to be entrepreneurs. We are instructed to be fruitful, multiply, fill the earth, subdue it, and have dominion. Some choose to do it and others never attempt to try. The true test and question are if we all have it, are you an Entrepreneur or a Want-repreneur?

I dedicate this work to everyone who dares to take the leap and be an entrepreneur, being fruitful, multiplying and having dominion in your area of enterprise. I dedicate this to you, the entrepreneur.

ACKNOWLEDGMENTS

THE CREATION OF THIS WORKBOOK HAS BEEN A REMARKABLE JOURNEY OF collaboration—a beautiful dance of minds and hearts coming together. I am beyond grateful for every soul that has touched these pages, adding their unique essence to its creation.

I must extend my heartfelt appreciation to Tinashe Hwande and Emmanuel Chriume, whose creativity and vision laid the solid foundation of this project. They did not just contribute; they sculpted, nurtured, and breathed life into the initial content. The depth and expansiveness of this workbook bear the mark of their genius.

Noel Hwande, your methodical approach brought clarity to our vision. Your precision and strategic insights have been instrumental in shaping the trajectory of this workbook with purpose and intention.

To all the entrepreneurs who have embraced this course, embarked on this journey, and committed to personal and professional growth: You are the heartbeat of this endeavor. It's because of your dedication, feedback, and shared experiences that this workbook is grounded in reality.

A special shoutout to Tanya and Tapiwa Gwaze. Your tenacity and drive are commendable. As you inch closer to that 7-Figure mark and set sights even higher, your journey serves as an inspiration and testament to what's possible.

Sandra Walters, coming from an esteemed background as an educator, you have imparted a crucial lesson. Through your wisdom, I've learned that to teach entrepreneurs effectively, one must employ the strategies and heart of teachers themselves. Your influence has been invaluable.

My cherished children, Tino, Tawanda, and Edem—you are the heartbeat behind every endeavor I undertake. Your love, resilience, and joy inspire me daily, reminding me of the generations we work to empower.

Finally, to my broader family and the support network surrounding me—you are the bedrock on which I stand. Your unwavering faith, encouragement, and shared enthusiasm have been my guiding stars.

I am deeply grateful for the collective dreams, dedication, and love that have woven this workbook into a tapestry of excellence. From the core of my being, thank you.

With boundless gratitude,

INTRODUCTION

How to Use This Workbook

At the end of each section, you will be asked to apply what you've learned by completing a 7-Figure Business Owner exercise. To ensure a clear understanding of the information, read one chapter per week to process the information effectively.

Exercise One: Quick Check for Understanding—The lines below "*Quick Check for Understanding*" reflect on the most relevant idea you understand in the part of the book. Complete a quick write about the most important focus within one sentence or a phrase.

Exercise Two: Apply What You've Learned Action Steps—During this exercise, you will take a deep dive into the information by developing their thoughts as you keep the ultimate goal in mind of becoming that 7-Figure Business Owner.

Final Exercise: 7 Figure Business Owner Strategic Business Plan—At that time, as the future 7-Figure Business Owner, you will create your own strategic plan. You may reflect back to previous tasks to prepare to take action while creating the business name, business overview, executive summary, business description, location, mission, vision, value, business objectives, identify problems, identify market and competitors, value proposition, marketing strategy, marketing business board, financial projections, your team, level structure, and create three simple goals.

CONTENTS

MY STORY

MY LIFE BEGAN IN THE MOST UNLIKELY PLACE. BORN AT THE TAIL END OF A violent civil war in what would eventually become the nation of Zimbabwe, I experienced first-hand the impact of renewing minds at a national level, but more importantly in my own family.

My parents, who had been forced to figure out how to work and raise children under a restrictive, segregated environment, suddenly had opportunities open up as independence came. So, with no hesitation, they did a deep dive into entrepreneurship as it was clear that they would be setting the tone and changing the perspective for their children and for generations to come.

From that point in 1980, I watched them struggle and strive in their entrepreneurship journey. Succeeding and failing and resetting. Gaining and losing wealth. Experiencing highs and lows. Looking back now, I am sure that the fact that they were only afforded a primary level education really disadvantaged them in their ability to scale and grow. At best, it was pure desperation and instinct that drove them.

My parents re-defined the term "multiple streams of income." They had multiple businesses at once, like clothing stores, a dry cleaner, record bar, photo studio, and a coffee shop, which were run out of the same storefront. Their retirement plan was investing in real estate.

Nevertheless, what I saw in them deeply influenced my own focus and approach to business. One funny story that comes to mind is that one of their businesses was to buy and sell used clothing. They would "ask" us kids to help sort and price these clothes for no pay. Little did they know that I had decided to, in effect, pay myself by stashing away some of these items of clothing, creating my own inventory and at the age of 16 years old, I was running a very profitable business selling used clothing to our homestead staff and others who worked in the surrounding neighborhoods. I even employed a debt collector and our gardener, Mukoma Thomas. I believe that is where my journey to seven figures truly began.

My name is Effie Hwande. I am an entrepreneur par excellence and devoted mother of three, and I have transformed challenges into steppingstones throughout my remarkable journey. Originating from Harare, Zimbabwe, I relocated to London at 18 to pursue nursing. This initial step was emblematic of my resilience; I overcame numerous hurdles both academically and personally, proving that adversity can shape formidable leaders.

My entrepreneurial tapestry is diverse and impactful. From establishing a nursing recruitment agency in my London residence to championing women's empowerment in Ghana through my skincare business and navigating the tech space in Silicon Valley and the agricultural sector in Zimbabwe, these ventures reflect my adaptability and vision. More than just a business narrative, my life is a testament to human tenacity, underscored by personal upheavals like international relocations, two divorces, bankruptcy, and confronting business challenges head-on.

Distinct from conventional business coaches, my audacious mission is to catalyze the inception of 1,000 businesses by 2025. As an entrepreneurial evangelist, I not only inspire but actively invest in the dreams of budding entrepreneurs.

We will look at my journey starting from the 9 to 5 and transitioning into entrepreneurship. The contents in this book will challenge you in whether you are an entrepreneur and look at the dynamics that can get you off course.

Complete these prompts with your inspiration for business.

I enjoy...

_____

_____

_____

_____

_____

My gift(s) is/are...

_____

_____

_____

_____

_____

I was born/raised to...

_____

_____

_____

_____

_____

BACKGROUND
Action Steps

Who are you? What is your gift or talent? What is your business story?
What made you interested in business? Where does that thought process
come from? Why is this business concept important?

_____

_____

_____

_____

_____

_____

_____

_____

_____

_____

_____

_____

_____

Chapter One

START WHERE YOU ARE

Are you a Want-repreneur or Entrepreneur?

I'VE HAD SEVERAL BUSINESS ATTEMPTS BEFORE THE FIRST SUCCESSFUL venture, and the lessons I learned the most were from the attempts that failed. I had a passion, but I forgot bills still needed to be paid. I walked away from my job and said, "I'm now focusing on my business," but I hadn't planned for it. The frustration eventually set in because bills had to be paid, so I dropped the passion and moved back to real life.

The question I ask of anyone who is going on this journey is, "Are you a want-repreneur or entrepreneur?" The difference between the two is one has been diligently preparing well. To be an entrepreneur you:

- ☐ Have a clear vision
- ☐ Set a pathway with objectives and targets
- ☐ Move forward in implementing the vision
- ☐ Have a Business Bank Account (not personal)
- ☐ Measure Progress using Key Performance Measures for your business performance and financial viability

The entrepreneur prepares to succeed while the want-repreneur is emotional and wants to magically obtain their goal. They think they work once and get paid for life, so the want-repreneur's mindset doesn't work. They say things like, "If only..., One of these days..." The want-repreneur "had" a brilliant idea, and years later they're still talking about it. Which one are you? Be honest with yourself.

Want-repreneur or Entrepreneur
Quick Check for Understanding:

_____

_____

_____

Taking the Leap from 9 to 5 to Entrepreneur

There are so many stories I can tell you about transitioning from the 9 to 5 into entrepreneurship. However, the one thing that sticks out the most was the shock of working 24 hours a day. I say that with a smile and a laugh because people have a misconception of being an entrepreneur.

Some believe since I'm self-employed I only work two hours a day. Yes, there will become a time when you've built the right structure with the right team where you may only be required to work two operational hours at a time.

However, the responsibilities are with you 24 hours a day, so the journey of transitioning from being an employee into an entrepreneur, in reality, brings challenging experiences. I had not anticipated the true responsibility of employing and managing people. The business grew quite quickly within a time of six months and the number of employees increased. I went from being an employee to entrepreneur, to being an employer, but I wasn't prepared for the endeavor. There was a lot of shock, horror, and learning to take place.

I chose to attend college in order to develop my leadership skills and financial management knowledge. The learning curve was steep, but those skills were important. As a new business owner, you cannot transition without being open to learning new strategies.

How do you take a leap from the 9 to 5 into being an entrepreneur? You must be prepared. You are better off being overprepared than under prepared. Take account of the true cost and transition. This will cost time and personnel resources, depending on your choice of industry. Do the research to identify the true cost of transferring from being the 9 to 5 employee into the entrepreneur you desire to be.

Steps for Preparation

1. Talk to your spouse or partner to be clear about your expectations.
2. Set aside money for the cost of living.
3. Make sure you have adequate finances to invest into the business for whatever is required.
4. Create the support structure and knowledge of the legalities, which are the requirements for starting this type of business.

Have a conversation with your significant other to ensure you're on the same page. Does he or she support you? Would you like to do it together? Make sure your mate can support you in this or your endeavor will be interrupted by relationship problems. If you're accustomed to two incomes, how are you going to make up the difference? You don't want him or her to feel burdened by your choice alone to go into business. If you are a business-minded person and you are single, this is something you need to discuss before tying the knot. You don't want your ambitious nature to interfere with your relationship. Be very clear. This is a risk management activity before it starts.

Determine the dollar amount needed to take the leap. Look at your budget and bills to figure out how much money is needed to cover your cost of living for six months before moving forward. Since this will affect the family, they should be included in the discussion if they are mature enough to share their thoughts.

The future 7-Figure Business Owner must do thorough research to determine the amount of money needed to invest in this new venture. As you continue to read, the information is laid out in upcoming chapters.

You will learn if becoming a sole proprietor is for you. However, a corporate structure protects its owner from being personally pursued for repayment of the company's debt and liabilities. This is called a limited liability corporation. There are so many resources available; simply research this information online. For example, the U.S. Small Business Administration in various cities helps individuals connect with business volunteers who share their experiences with future business owners. Tap into available SBA SCORE for free mentorship by retired executives in your industry. Obtain practical advice about registering your business and be clear on your tax responsibilities. Speak with experts in this field for more in-depth understanding. This will help you make sure your formal structure is in place and correct. Getting this right is important.

Once you decide to take the leap, it will feel uncomfortable at first, but get out of your comfort zone and make this huge commitment. Next, communicate with your family, count the cost with time, resources, and money. Make a plan and set aside finances and/or raise the money to fund the vision. Find your networking group or groups and engage. Prepare for success!

Taking the Leap
Quick Check for Understanding:

_____

_____

_____

Figuring Out a Failure

Finally, current business owners or people with a side hustle should look at the financial aspect. If you've done something for a long time, and the business still isn't generating any income, that's a failure. When you've done a task seemingly well, but you are frustrated by the outcome, this can also be considered a form of failure. When you have not been clear in your planning, the ending results may turn out to be a form of failure. This is far from what you intended.

A successful business is measured by results, which is financial. Therefore, evaluate with measurable goals, so your success is obvious. If you put in time, commitment, dedication, and you suffer a loss, this isn't considered success. Successful results should calculate as a profit after all of the expenses are paid. My experiences with failure are many to be honest. There are opportunities I have taken in business that have not worked out. A lot of money has been invested, commitments have been made, and the end product wasn't delivered.

When you know the business is failing, you may desire to keep pushing because you believe the tipping point might be about to happen. However, tell yourself this is as far as it needs to go and move on to something else. Failure is a blessing in itself.

Sometimes business ideas fail because there wasn't a strong enough market. You simply had a passion or hobby you wanted to turn into a business. So yes, this is a hobby that you love to do, but when the costs outweigh your resources because they are limited, or there is no financial return, that's a huge problem. So how do you turn your failure into success?

My most recent failure was taking numerous resources, finances, and creating a team. I pushed for a number of years, even though there was revenue, and the business failed to become profitable. The turning point occurred when we identified not having the human resources required to turn things around, so going into a management partnership was the solution. I moved from that expectation of being 100% owner into a partnership, and this was structured in such a way that all parties would benefit from the success.

This was the turning point in my attempts to build a successful business. What are the takeaways from the failure? I think we beat ourselves up when things go wrong. You must applaud yourself for being courageous enough to get started. You began the journey. The failure can result in some good things. You possibly formed relationships along the way, which may allow you to have access to resources that you wouldn't have had before. Use that failure to say *maybe this is not what I really want to do now.* You've given this business a shot, but you have a chance to revisit what is important and begin something new.

It's never too late. I read an article where it said older people are more successful when establishing a business, or they are more likely to succeed in whatever they set out to do. I think there's an element of truth in this because there's a level of maturity that failure brings. They offer maturity in the sense that they have experience in assessing where things have gone wrong. Then they determine if it can be fixed and learn from the mistakes. Their maturity urges them not to fall into those same pitfalls again. These business owners move on in the process and aren't paralyzed by trial and error.

Figuring Out a Failure
Quick Check for Understanding:

_____

_____

_____

Burn the Boat

Learn to burn the boat. Many people will embark on an opportunity with plan B, C, and D as the safety net. Personally, I think that when you do that, you're not fully committed to the original plan. You have to get to a place where you learn to burn the boat. I remember leaving a great job, which was paying so well. This position came with benefits, but I had to say, "No." I wanted the opportunity of being an entrepreneur starting my own business.

Even though there was so much talk around my network and my circle of influence, the people that matter in my life asked, "Why do you need to leave all this to go into the great unknown?" But I had already decided within myself to begin the journey, so I planned to burn the boat. I had to lay aside everything that made me comfortable because each step of the way there was no coming back.

I started off by reducing my hours at work to three days a week. This meant I focused on working efficiently with less hours and less income. In 24 hours, I finished my work 9 to 5, and I started working on my business after the children went to bed from 8:00 p.m. until the early morning. I became consumed with the vision in my heart, and I could tangibly feel the success in my being. I was motivated to keep going and stay focused.

Don't hold back. Burn the boat and move into that opportunity wholeheartedly. Refuse to look back. How can you burn the boat and focus on that new business opportunity? You can start by making sure that you have enough savings. Have at least three months of living expenses if you are in a business that can generate income very quickly. If not, save for at least six months. That will give you the peace of mind to say *I'm okay with my day-to-day living expenses*. Alternatively, you can cut back on living expenses by living with family who are supportive of your vision and will assist with the costs of living while you build your business. Whatever it takes, commit to planning well and proceed.

Remember, the reason some of my business ventures failed in the past was I completely overlooked that bills still needed to be paid at the end of each month because I was determined to get started. Make sure you have enough funds. If not, make sure you have support during the start-up stage. This offers you the ability not to have financial strain. Make the changes you need to and get started on implementing your vision.

It's difficult to have vision and be excited about a new opportunity when you're thinking about your bills, expenses, the cost of living, and the challenges that come. Your mind should be totally on building the business. Don't research to the point of procrastinating. Sometimes people overdo the researching and talk themselves out of starting, so don't arrest yourself by over analyzing. Ensure you have adequate information about the opportunity and move forward as you structure your business.

Have an ability to measure your progress. On a weekly basis, do reflective thoughts of how productive you were this week. What did I set out to achieve? Have I achieved it? If I haven't, why not? What was I able to achieve? What do I need to improve the upcoming week? If it's outside of my control, like a supplier or another third party, then maybe I need to look for a different supplier or a different resource. If I don't have adequate resources available, then how can I find those resources? I need to find the resources within the time needed. How can I keep track of the time I've set to achieve? Do I have a way of doing some reflective thoughts on a regular basis at the end of each day? Have I used my time well at the end of the week? Have I achieved what I set out to do? If not, what adjustments do I need to make?

Now that you know you have clarity of purpose for an entrepreneurship. You have prepared for success enough to take the leap. It's time to burn the boat.

Burn the Boat
Quick Check for Understanding:

_____

_____

_____

Chapter One

ACTION STEPS

Apply What You've Learned

Want-repreneur or Entrepreneur?

Directions: On each side of the T-chart, write the characteristics that describe the individual.

WANT-REPRENEUR	ENTREPRENEUR

List your clear vision and pathway with objectives and targets. How have you moved forward or plan to do so? Identify your business bank account or get one. How do you measure progress using key performance measures?

_____

_____

_____

_____

_____

_____

_____

Taking the Leap from your 9 to 5?

What are your thoughts about taking the leap from your 9 to 5? Write each step to make this happen. Create an exit strategy that works for you. Do not allow this to paralyze you.

_____

_____

_____

_____

_____

_____

_____

_____

_____

_____

_____

_____

Burn the Boat

Are you willing to burn the boat? What does burn the boat mean to you? What steps must you take to move forward? List them below.

_____

_____

_____

_____

_____

_____

_____

_____

_____

_____

_____

_____

Face Your Fears

What comes to mind as you think about failure? Call out your fears by listing them below as they come to your mind.

_____

_____

_____

_____

_____

_____

_____

_____

_____

_____

_____

_____

Encourage Yourself

Encourage yourself by creating a playlist of encouraging music, listen to your favorite encourager, or look at videos that prompt you to encourage yourself. Use the space below to remind yourself that you can do anything you set your mind to.

_____

_____

_____

_____

_____

_____

_____

_____

_____

What are your 3 take-aways from this session?

1. _____

_____

_____

_____

2. _____

_____

_____

_____

3. _____

_____

_____

_____

WORKING WITH WHAT YOU HAVE

Work Ethic

WHAT EXACTLY DOES IT MEAN? IT'S THE ACCOUNTABILITY AND FLEXIBILITY TO adapt to changes. Developing a work ethic is fundamental and critical to a successful business or any initiative you embark on. For example, even in school, you must have the work ethic to study well while preparing for your exams. The same principles apply in business. You must understand: Where you are going? What resources are needed? Who to partner with? Reflect on the process while you get to the planned destination. Evaluate along the way. The abilities for where you're headed can change as you proceed, so it's okay to make adjustments sometimes. Determining whether you succeeded or not should be clear.

Work Ethic
Quick Check for Understanding:

_____

_____

_____

Resourceful

How do you become resourceful? There are so many creative ways of maximizing with the little that you have. Really maximizing on the little that you have at any given time and turning it around for a greater good.

For instance, I wanted to work in the advertising industry, but I was a certified nurse with nursing experience. I reached out to a company that I desired to work for, but they weren't hiring at the time. Therefore, I contacted the most senior person relentlessly. I called and asked to speak to that individual, but they would say he was not available. And I called again, and they repeated, "He's not available." Eventually when I called, I said, "Okay, I understand you're not hiring at the moment, but would you give me an opportunity to come and volunteer in your organization?" And they replied, "Yes." I was so committed, dedicated, and helpful in every sense that a position was created for me. That's how you can be resourceful.

In the business world, Jamie Kern Lima exemplifies resourcefulness. At a pivotal moment for her company, Jamie Kern Lima showcased the epitome of resourcefulness through authentic marketing. Recognizing the need to connect with women who faced similar skin issues, she diverged from the industry standard of featuring flawless, airbrushed models during her QVC segment.

Instead, Lima opted for an array of models who varied in age and had real complexion challenges, effectively turning perceived imperfections into powerful selling points. This innovative approach resonated deeply with viewers, allowing Lima to sell out her product inventory within minutes. Her ability to creatively leverage authenticity as a resource led not only to immediate sales but also to the long-term success of IT Cosmetics, demonstrating the transformative power of being resourceful in business.

So, what does it mean to be resourceful? Being resourceful means having the ability to find quick and clever ways to overcome challenges, solve problems, and make the most out of available resources. It's about being adaptable, flexible, and proactive, especially when faced with difficult situations or limited means. Resourcefulness is not just about using what you have, but also about maximizing your potential and leveraging your skills, tools, and relationships in innovative ways.

Remember if you're clear about what you want to achieve, you can make it happen. Let's say you are going into the beauty sector. You must have access to your market, so you could start by approaching a store that sell a variety of products, which could be your competing product. You can go and volunteer your services or apply for a job. So not only are you an employee, but you have also been given access to the market. This allows you to understand people's buying habits. That gives you the full one-on-one exposure to the trends or things that your potential customers may find interest in. Start from where you are, and you will go a long way.

Resourceful
Quick Check for Understanding:

_____

_____

_____

Taking Risks

I have so many stories about taking risks, but as I've gotten older, my risks have become more calculated in the sense that I now spend more time researching before I take the risk, but taking risks is that first step of coming out of your comfort zone. You have to do it. So many people talk themselves out of an opportunity because they are afraid, or they have someone else talk them out of it. Anything that you decide to do in the space of becoming an entrepreneur requires you to be ready to take risks. You must take risks.

From the time I left Zimbabwe, going to London with no real plan in place was a significant risk. Then enrolling into nursing school when my parents thought I should be a lawyer or in another career, was another risk. Starting a business without a lot of money to get started. Moving to a new country at the age of 50—that's a huge risk. Packing up my bags to travel for a new opportunity was a risk. My life story is filled and punctuated with so many risks taken. Through all of those risks, I have become that 7-Figure Business Owner. I have no regrets. There have been challenges and difficulties along the way, but no regrets.

This topic makes me think about how Tyler Perry's transformation from homelessness to Hollywood success is a vivid illustration of the power of taking risks and venturing into the unknown. After a failed stage play left him sleeping in his car, Perry could have easily succumbed to self-doubt and given up on his dreams.

Instead, he chose to reinvest in his vision, re-staging the play with adjustments based on past lessons and audience feedback. This bold, risky move turned his fortunes around, eventually leading to a string of successful productions and a multimedia empire. Perry's journey underscores the transformative potential of releasing past failures and self-defeating beliefs to seize new, risky opportunities.

Taking Risks
Quick Check for Understanding:

_____

_____

_____

Chapter Two

ACTION STEPS

Apply What You've Learned

Work Ethic

Who are you accountable to? How well do you adapt to changes? How do or did you develop a strong work ethic? What is considered a strong work ethic in your eyes? Is it learned or something you are born with? What are the benefits of a strong work ethic?

_____

_____

_____

_____

_____

_____

_____

_____

_____

Directions: Place examples of a strong ethic vs. poor work ethic.

STRONG WORK ETHIC	POOR WORK ETHIC

Resourceful

List your resources. Add additional circles to describe the benefits, in detail, and write any resources that you can barter or volunteer to learn.

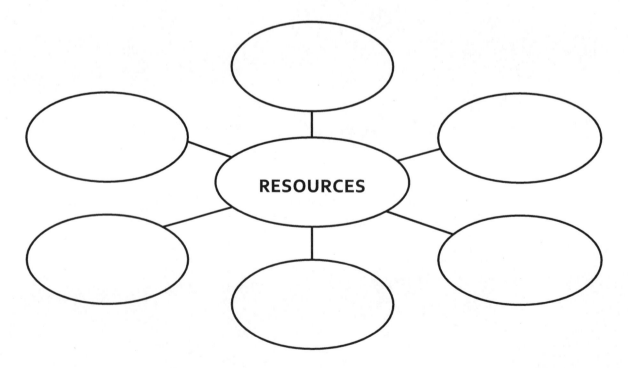

Taking Risks

What risks have you taken? What does it look like to take risks and have them pay off?

RISK TAKEN	RESULTS

What is the cost of not taking risks? What does it look like to take risks in your life right now? What's the best that could happen?

_____

_____

_____

_____

_____

_____

_____

What are your 3 take-aways from this session?

1. _____

_____

_____

_____

2. _____

_____

_____

_____

3. _____

_____

_____

_____

Chapter Three

THE MIND BEHIND THE 7-FIGURE BUSINESS OWNER

IN THIS SECTION OF THE COURSE, WE WILL COVER THE MINDSET OF THE 7-FIGURE BUSINESS OWNER and discover every aspect of the mindset. As we explore, things may jog your memory with thoughts that plague your mind. I will introduce skills that can help you master your mind. You must become a 7-Figure Business Owner in your mind before it manifests. The attitude needed to engage in longevity and the ability to succeed in starting and growing your business begins with your vision.

Mind Behind the 7-Figure Business Owner
Quick Check for Understanding:

_____

_____

_____

Renewing Your Mind

Going into business once the decision has been made is an exciting and yet nervous experience for most people. It's exciting because you are setting out on this journey that you have imagined for yourself, and you're looking forward to the things ahead. However, it's also nerve-wracking because of the great unknown.

But the one thing that gives me peace continually is the scripture Romans 12:2 where it says, "Be transformed by the renewing of your mind so you may test that which is good, acceptable and pleasing to God." The passage talks a lot about not being conformed to a certain way of thinking, behavior, and way of conducting yourself. You can be transformed by continuously renewing your mind and always testing. So, the question is, "How am I lining up with the principles and my beliefs? Am I offering a good quality service to my customers? Am I doing it with the integrity and at the level of quality that I would expect for myself and my family? Are my offerings the same quality to others? Does it line up with what is good and pleasing?"

Also, you must have an awareness that you're not always the best solution, and that's okay. They may be unhappy with your service or product, so have the ability to receive feedback and learn from it. Renewing your mind daily means you're not fixed on being right. Therefore, you're open to receiving all levels of feedback and responses to improve, perfect, and get better at what you do.

What is the mindset of the 7-Figure Business Owner? The 7-Figure Business Owner makes these positive affirmations daily to renew his or her mind.

Daily Positive Business Affirmations

1. I continuously renew by confronting the fears that I have on a daily basis. Each day I acknowledge the fears and replace them with the success ahead.

2. I confront the naysayers in my life by recognizing they're there, but I don't allow their voices to drown the vision and desire I have to succeed. My mindset is relentless.

3. I am dedicated and committed to fulfilling what I set out to do.

4. I look to people who have succeeded in the industry, not for validation but support to have access to resources that help me focus on the areas I must concentrate on.

5. I acknowledge my shortcomings, and I set out to do the work. But it may not work out exactly how I planned. I take experiences into my plan or consider challenges as lessons learned.

6. I forge ahead in spite of the challenges.

7. I succeed by staying on top of my mind. I conquer my fears by casting down the thoughts that introduce negative ideas like, *You're not good enough. You're not worthy.* I must remind myself that I refuse to fail.

Review your plan regularly to rehearse your strategic plan.

Renewing Your Mind
Quick Check for Understanding:

_____

_____

_____

Overcoming Mental Distractions

Keepers and Wasters

There are habits you must keep that lead to success, and some habits waste time, so they must be thrown away because they undermine your success. They stop you from achieving. Equally, there are people you must keep, and there are people that you need to let go. I can come up with so many examples of both habits and people that I've had to set aside in order to fulfil the plans and purposes that I have set to achieve.

Some of the habits I've had to throw away include procrastination. You may have a great idea and have done your research to the full, but you keep coming up with a reason why this isn't the right time to get started. That's procrastination because you already have the tools and the business plan completed. You're ready to get started. Keep moving forward. Don't stop.

The people who are wasters are the ones that leave you weighted. If you have a discussion with them, you come out of that conversation even more overwhelmed, fearful, unsure, and uncertain. They don't bring anything good, just a lot of negativity. When a person is starting a business, you don't need that level of disapproval. You're already going against the grain by stepping out into something new or building from a small scale and making it a formal business from a hobby. You don't need that negativity around you. People will say it's going to fail or what if this goes wrong? Or have you considered this, that, and the other? All of these things are already occupying your mind, so you don't need external forces adding to and building this ideology. People must be let go and habits have to die.

Over the years, I've learned there are people in my life who are there for the long run. They are mostly family members who are fully vested, and they'll support me. They cheer me on by being present and seeing the good in all that I'm trying to do. Then, there are certain people who are there for a specific time or reason to motivate you or the team by offering a solution when you need it to help you reach your company's objectives. However, they're not meant to be there for the long haul, and I've learned over the years once the purpose has been accomplished, the dynamics of the relationship changes. This is when I know it's time to let go and move on.

Maturity taught me better ways of managing relationships. In the past, I was more cutthroat. For example, I was impatient in managing poor performance to the extent of having conversations like, "Hey, your time's up. Thank you so much. You've been great, but you aren't who we need!"

However, with maturity and the wisdom that comes from so many attempts and trying different things, I understand everything is relational, so it's important to start and end things well. Therefore, I learned to be an excellent communicator. I believe somethings come to an end, so I don't hold on to things or people. I don't take offense, and I've learned to move on quickly.

Keepers and wasters also apply to your day to day in terms of your well-being. We've talked about the mindset. There's also the wellness of body. I have taken up greater levels of exercise because I realize that it's not only about being focused on the strategy and the business. You must take care of yourself, so I had to work on my health, eating habits, and exercise. All of this creates who I am as a whole person. Your relationships, spiritual life, faith, and family are all subsections of your well-being. How you handle all parts of your life affect your welfare overall.

Determine if there are things that are "keepers" and "wasters" in your life. Most people know who or what's wasting their time, but they don't want to acknowledge it. If you have been sitting around for years planning to start a business, and you're not actually doing anything, then stop talking and take action. Move from the thought, *Oh, I wish I could do that*, to actually doing it and measuring the steps taken.

Accountability partners are critical because these individuals have been given permission to advise and speak into a specific area of your life. I have health, exercise, and business accountability partners. Your business accountability partner will understand your objective, what you're setting up to achieve, the timeline, milestones within that process, and the output you're striving to achieve.

The accountability process questions a person's attentiveness to the tasks that have been set. The individuals have the right to speak into areas where a business owner is failing or may be slacking. With this permission, the partners may give constructive feedback and criticism, so it's a safe place to be vulnerable. It has been important to have accountability partners throughout my life, and this makes such a difference by adding to my ability to reflect on success and failure from an independent position.

You may ask, how do I find accountability partners, even in these uncertain times? Reach out to experts in various industries. Many people will support by offering resource materials for you to use. In addition to that, the 7-Figure Business Owner created a support group where you can come in and have accountability partners that will assist you in every stage of your growth or development process. If you're starting out and need different levels of accountability, that resource is available. There are so many things you can tap into at **effiemedia.com**.

Destiny helpers represent the miracles of the hand of God. For example, calling a real estate investor with an impressive portfolio who will offer you an hour of their time is an example of a Destiny partner. As you sit with him or her and are given the freedom to ask all the questions you have as you embark on your journey, that's a Destiny helper because this individual isn't obligated to help you. I'm surrounded by them. They are people who see the greater good in what you're trying to do, and they have the ability to give you a directive to say, "Try this. Speak to this person. Have you heard about this? Read this." They are helping you accelerate your achievement. Destiny helpers have been miracles and blessings in disguise through the course of my business journey.

Keepers and Wasters
Quick Check for Understanding:

_____

_____

_____

Other People's Opinions

Other people's opinions have a time and place, but not all the time. You will find the minute that you make yourself available either in a service industry or in a product industry, you have the attention of your customer base. That opens you up to a lot of scrutiny and a lot of critiquing. If you're not careful, you can be overwhelmed by the opinions of others to the point of being stunted in moving forward. Do not get stifled by the opinions of others.

That's why it's important to be clear about why you're doing what you're doing. Is there a problem for which you're providing a solution? The solution has to be greater than the noise around you.

Consider the journey of products like Viagra and Post-it Notes. Viagra, initially researched as a treatment for heart-related chest pain, found its fame and approval as a solution for erectile dysfunction. On the other hand, Post-it Notes were the result of a failed attempt to develop a super-strong adhesive. Both products might not have achieved their initial goals, but they discovered new, often more significant purposes along the way.

If you are not careful, other people's opinions can be so overwhelming that you don't move forward, so you end up abandoning the idea. I remember one or two things that I was so clear I wanted to do, and I was ready to proceed. But someone who was close and dear spoke a word of caution or questioned my ability to succeed. Then, this starts to have an impact on my urgency. Therefore, be cautious about other people's opinions and take it with a pinch of salt. Keep moving forward.

I'm good with setting boundaries. I don't have a problem with that. I respectfully say thank you for your opinion. I've heard it; however, I'm moving forward with what I've decided to do. It's not to be arrogant or pompous, but it's on the basis that I've done my research. I have established what I'm doing is the right course of action and there's a market for me to provide a service to, so I'm moving forward with implementation. Sometimes the people that are within our own circle of influence like loved ones, family, and friends have a sense of fear. They don't want to see us fail, and this fear can be communicated through opinions that can dampen the planning you may have put in place already.

Opinions of other people matter when they're coming from a good place. If there is someone who has achieved what you're trying to do and they can give you a word of caution, receive it as such, but don't stop moving forward. Evaluate the feedback that you're getting and determine whether or not it's valid for you. Someone's failure will not necessarily result in your failure. If someone tried to do what you're attempting and failed, figure out why that is. Use the information to reinforce your plan and make sure you have a good foundation. Do all of your due diligence before you move forward.

Other People's Opinions
Quick Check for Understanding:

_____

_____

_____

Overcoming Fear of Failure

Overcoming the fear of failure is deciding to create the business anyway. The fear of failure can be born out of so many things. You may have examples. I recall examples of my parents as entrepreneurs. They had highs and lows in their business journey, so I developed a fear because of that. I didn't want to fail as I reflected on those days. This can be ingrained in you from past experiences. Fear can come from not knowing what tomorrow will bring, but have enough faith and confidence in what you're doing.

Once you determine and establish there's a market, you must be present, continue to review, and push. Fear is a healthy thing as well. There are times when it keeps you grounded to what's important for your business. When you are too self-assured, you become arrogant and can talk yourself out of your business, so there has to be a healthy balance of *Am I doing the right thing?* This causes a person to continuously improve on what they're doing, so it's not an unhealthy fear of devastation. Evaluate yourself with questions: Am I applying myself? Am I still listening to my customers? Am I providing the level of service or product quality that I committed to? If not, how can I fix that?

Do it anyway. You owe it to yourself! How does fear disguise itself? Fear can disguise itself as a thought that says, It's not the right time. It's not the right place. You need to try something else. Fear can present in so many different ways, and you can talk yourself out of a really good business opportunity. I've had experiences where people will question. People around me would ask, "Are you sure that this is really what you want to do? I don't think this is the time. Look at where you are. You have a young family, and you don't have the time to concentrate on this."

You know for sure while you're alone, but the minute someone comes to cast fear or doubt into your situation, you aren't sure. If you're not assured by the research and actions taken to be prepared, you can easily talk yourself out of and miss the reality of a successful business or the opportunity that you've always wanted. If you don't move forward, you become resentful. So, you owe it to yourself to get started. Talk yourself out of the fear and proceed. What if you've tried and failed in the business that you started? Then you learn from that process and uncover why this venture has not succeeded.

Perhaps your intentions were misguided, or your planning was inadequate. It either didn't work out in terms of the relationships created by the partnership or you didn't fully get the product requirements. Stop beating yourself up about it. Decide where you went wrong and make corrections. Learn from the experience and keep moving forward. This is a must.

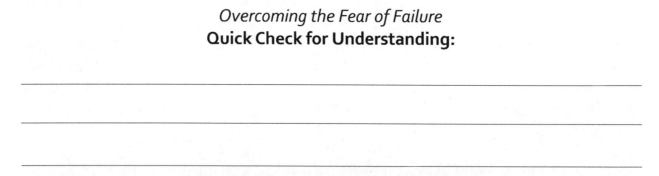

Overcoming the Fear of Failure
Quick Check for Understanding:

Maintaining the Renewed Mindset

Single-Minded Focus

A single-minded focus is critical to success. Identify what you want to do, and cut out all the noise, disturbance—anything that can get in the way of that focus. I've been known to call people and say, "Hey, I won't be available for a period of time because I'm focusing on achieving a specific goal."

There are things you can put into place to make sure you have single-minded focus. You may exercise as a way of starting your day just to rejuvenate your mind and get yourself ready for what's ahead. Prioritize things on your To-Do List daily and cross out things you accomplish. Sometimes when I'm out running and I don't feel like running, each mile I complete I say to myself, *Well done*, because I need to be encouraged even more when I don't feel like doing so.

When it comes to business, there are monotonous tasks that must be done daily. These things create successful businesses, but if they aren't tended to, then you're creating something that has cracks in the foundation. You will not build a business that will last. A 7-Figure Business requires owners to train their minds in the things that are important for that time.

While people prepare for an exam, they typically focus on reviewing all they've learned up to that point. Before taking the exam, they simply refresh and prepare for it. Everything else comes after that. So, in the same way, when you're starting a business, identify the things that are critical for you to be successful. Launch the tasks that are critical from the beginning, which is needed to continue throughout a start-up business. Train your mind to focus on being committed, making sure you achieve everything you set out to do.

For example, I applied myself in terms of having a single-minded focus by telling family and friends that for a period of time they will not have access to me as they normally would. I was locked into preparing for the business concept I signed up for. I would say, "I am preparing to launch a business and completing a very important task, so for that reason, there will be a course of study I'm working on." I explain to them that I love them, but I will not be available to socialize for the next six to nine months; I'm here and focused.

Most of my family will tell you on the day I complete the exam or the day I have my certification done, I pick up the phone and say, "Hey, I'm done. Let's sit down and have dinner to reconnect." Therefore, it's okay to take yourself out of a space to focus on what you set your mind to achieve. Being focused and finishing is important to what you set out to do. Every minute counts.

I believe time is to all equally, and it's the most significant, valuable, and expensive resource we have. Each person has been given 24 hours in a day, but how we utilize that time is different. I measure carefully how I spend my time, so I will appoint myself a completion deadline. I assign times when I log through my calendar, write in my journal, and take break times. Including rest times is extremely important. I account for every minute and every second. Being focused is having the ability to identify the tasks that you are good at doing and delegating the things that take you longer to do.

For instance, if I had to create a logo or design a concept, I could do it, but this would take me weeks to months. Yet for a very low cost, I can have an expert create the design. I will give them the idea of what I'm trying to achieve, and they can put together the concepts and the visuals for me to decide between two or three different finished products. Then, I select the one that works best for me, so this allows me to be mindful of how I use my time.

Organize the use of your time, and focus on the critical tasks ahead as a business owner, which include the strategy of understanding the market. The 7-Figure Business Owner attends to things that he or she has the ability to complete, not the things he or she wants to do.

Single-Minded Focus
Quick Check for Understanding:

_____

_____

_____

Time Management

The importance of time management and having an awareness of what this really means is one of the founding principles of success in business. Get to a place where you understand the value of your time. When I did research on people who are successful in the different sectors of my personal interest, I found they will not waste their time on activities that don't generate an outcome or make their business more viable. They come up with a system of delegation, not to undermine the importance of every task, but they conduct an assessment to determine where their value rests. In the process, they delegate tasks to others, so it's important to have the ability to manage your time. Every minute and every second counts because each second costs.

The importance of time management and comprehending its genuine value is a cornerstone of business success. Bill Gates, the co-founder of Microsoft, serves as a testament to this principle. He is known to value his time meticulously. In the early days of Microsoft, Gates was involved in many aspects of the business, from coding to marketing. But as the company grew, he recognized the importance of delegation to ensure he could focus on where he added the most value. Gates once remarked, "No matter how much money you have, you can't buy more time."

This encapsulates the essence of his philosophy. By assessing and recognizing where his true value lay, he could delegate other tasks, ensuring that every second was spent in the most impactful way. It's not about diminishing the significance of any task but about realizing where your unique contribution makes the most difference. Thus, mastering time management isn't just about productivity; it's about understanding the worth of every ticking moment.

At the start of many of my business ventures, there wasn't a great deal of money to invest until I had adequate resources. This allows owners to outsource or grow by bringing more people in, and this costs. I think the cost is more evident in the ability to be productive, so the fact that I had to do everything limited my ability to be productive faster.

The process of being productive was hindered. For example, I would sit down and write all the policies and procedures myself. I wrote all the processes and wanted to have a say in everything. But eventually I realized there's a fee to be paid; however, by outsourcing to establish policies and procedures, I could pay a company a small fee, which had a good payment plan. This allowed my company the ability to be compliant in the requirements of the sector more efficiently. Outsourcing various tasks allowed me to get the business started, and I was able to stay up to date with any changes in regulations.

Sometimes we think we're saving money by utilizing the time to do the task ourselves. However, this interferes with the production, which becomes overwhelming and creates inefficiencies and financial losses.

Therefore, I designed a workload time management tool. It's a very simple table with different sections. This graphic organizer starts with the date, the day of the week, time of the task, the people needed, and the time spent. When I do that for a week, I know how I'm using the majority of my time in the operational components.

From this exercise, I learned that I was not doing the business well, even possibly losing productive time. To manage the process, I use a time tracker to hold myself accountable. This activity is extremely valuable to see where you're busy and where you're being productive by tracking the time. I use this weekly to understand how I'm using my time.

Most business owners are looking at the effectiveness and efficiency within each department or team, like if there's a change in the service that we provide or if we have a higher number of complaints or compliments coming through. It helps us determine how we're using our time and how resourceful we are as an organization, and utilizing the time tracker can guide your whole structure as a business. This tool will help you understand the level of support that you need administratively, operationally, and in any other section of your business. Also, it will help you manage the expectations of having a larger team.

The time tracker is still an effective tool if you're working by yourself. If you're working by yourself, the tracker can be used to evaluate how you spend your time on certain days. I will see I spent 80% of my time doing these tasks and 20% with my customers. However, I'm supposed to be spending more time focused on my customers, quality, and improvement of the service or product I'm selling. Be honest with yourself about how you use your time and how you can improve. Time is of the essence, and missed opportunities happen because of not reviewing the process.

For example, slow responses to customers make your customers upset by delaying or not providing a service. You lose the window of opportunity because you haven't planned well, and your time management is lacking.

Time Management
Quick Check for Understanding:

_____

_____

_____

Chapter Three

ACTION STEPS

Apply What You've Learned

The Mind

How does the 7-Figure Business Owner renew his or her mind?

_____

_____

_____

_____

_____

_____

_____

_____

_____

_____

Keeper /Waster

Evaluate the Keepers and Wasters in your life and list them on the chart.

KEEPERS	WASTERS

People's Opinions

What experiences do you have with people sharing their opinions? How did you respond after hearing their ideas?

_____

_____

_____

_____

_____

_____

_____

Overcoming Fear

What makes you fearful? What past experiences cause you to be fearful? What daily actions must you take to overcome?

_____

_____

_____

_____

_____

What's On Your Mind?

Directions: On this graffiti wall, design a creation that represents the things on your mind. You may use words, drawing, and color.

Single-Minded

How do you think you'll benefit from being single-minded?

_____

_____

_____

_____

_____

_____

_____

_____

_____

_____

_____

_____

Workload Time Management Tool

DATE	DAY OF WEEK	TIME	TASK	PEOPLE INVOLVED	TIME SPENT COMPLETING TASK

What are your 3 take-aways from this session?

1. _____

_____

_____

_____

2. _____

_____

_____

_____

3. _____

_____

_____

_____

Chapter Four

FUNDAMENTALS OF CREATING A BUSINESS

WE WILL LOOK AT THE FUNDAMENTALS OF CREATING A BUSINESS. THIS covers the critical areas for developing the business plan, which include a level of research and analysis needed to determine a viable business strategy. The ability to analyze as you go through the journey of structuring your business and learning the importance of working in partnerships while collaborating with others are key.

Over the years and in the many businesses I have established, I've come to recognize that there are non-negotiable principles for creating a business. More than just drafting a business plan, it's the deep dive into research, the constant checking, and adjusting as we go along. So, let's go through these principles as I break down the seven key pillars that have been foundational in my success. Whether it's the magic of genuine partnerships or the need to always be ready to adapt, each of these elements has a story to tell, and a lesson to teach. Ready to dive in?

The Seven Pillars of Creating a Business

1. **Research:** This is more than just a quick search online. The future business owner immerses in exhaustive study—understanding competitors, identifying and grasping the pulse of the target audience, and anticipating potential roadblocks.

7-FIGURE
BUSINESS OWNER
PILLARS OF SUCCESS

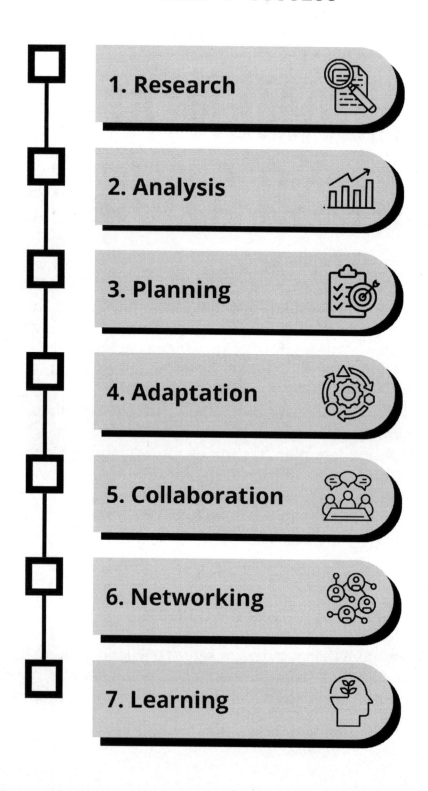

1. Research

2. Analysis

3. Planning

4. Adaptation

5. Collaboration

6. Networking

7. Learning

2. **Analysis:** Here, we sift through the research data, using time-tested tools like Strengths, Weaknesses, Opportunities, and Threats (SWOT) Analysis, ensuring we know our strengths and areas that need boosting.

3. **Planning:** I've always believed in having a business plan a clear blueprint that lays down our ambitions, strategies, and of course, the financial groundwork and goals for the road ahead.

4. **Adaptation:** In my journey, I've learned that businesses are a bit like life— unpredictable. The key to succeeding lies in how swiftly we pivot, embrace fresh insights, and adapt to unexpected turns.

5. **Collaboration:** Identifying and establishing fruitful partnerships have been my gold. It's about valuing and synergizing with others, both within and outside the business.

6. **Networking:** This is more than just exchanging business cards. I have an innate knack for recognizing synergies between people and businesses. It's about creating meaningful connections, introducing individuals who can mutually benefit, and fostering collaborations that amplify success.

7. **Learning:** In my life, I've made it a point to learn continuously. I'm always driven by understanding what fuels people's passion to build thriving businesses. Mentoring and coaching diverse individuals across various industries has not only been a joy but also a rich learning experience for me. Their insights and stories constantly teach me and keep my finger on the pulse of the business world.

Having learned the fundamental pillars that have been instrumental in my entrepreneurial journey, it's time to take the next step. Let's discuss and navigate the intricacies of how to effectively transform this knowledge into actionable success.

Pillars of Success
Quick Check for Understanding:

_____

_____

_____

Planning for Success

How do you plan for success? Remove fear by having a solid foundation. A solid foundation comes from robust systems and processes. As mentioned previously, I have a business in a sector that is highly regulated. At first, I wanted to write all the policies and procedures, but it would fail eventually because regulations and legislation change on a regular basis, and I wasn't even aware of some of the changes.

Therefore, I had to learn from early on that I was better off hiring a legal organization that was in the business of staying up to date with the laws. This expert legal organization created all the policies and procedures. They made sure my company stayed compliant by creating a solid foundation for our business.

In order to have success, create a foundation that can cater to short-, medium-, and long-term business growth and review along the way to remind yourself that you're continuing down the right path. You should be achieving the things you've set out to do. A part of planning well is determining what is the solution or improvement you're bringing to the industry. Stay on top of what you do well. Are you bringing a solution to the industry? You can be excellent at what you do; however, if it isn't a solution, you will have no customers. Make sure there is a need and/or problem for which your business is the solution.

Originally, I desired to create a nursing staffing agency with ten highly skilled and qualified nurses to be a part of a team that served within a multidisciplinary group. Years later, as the business has grown, this desire still remains the same, but on a larger scale.

I was clear on the vision and as a team, we knew what we wanted to do was different, and we've scaled up. However, there are times when business owners get this wrong, or maybe the dynamic of the team is not suited for the client group or whatever it is. Use your time to evaluate and decide if those actions didn't work. What can work, or how can you improve? There has to be a process of continuous improvement, but don't become so lethargic to the point you grow too big, or you no longer care about the small things. Don't fall asleep and say, "We don't do those things." Don't become extinct because you didn't pay attention to the minor things or where the industry was going.

Success Planning
Quick Check for Understanding:

_____

_____

_____

Skip the Passion... Find the Need

Find a need. What do I mean by skip the passion? Sometimes passion gets in the way of practical application. Take a pragmatic approach and deal with the issues sensibly and realistically. Count the cost. Work out what you are going to do and get on with it. Flipping a hobby into a business requires a certain level of discipline. Apply yourself and do it well. Be accountable in the process.

Some processes don't transfer well into a business. Are you able to take that critique? Maybe you are somewhat of a perfectionist. If someone speaks to you on a regular basis as a business owner and advises you, you could save a lot of time by creating some checks and balances to free your time and focus on growing your business.

The process of doing business like a hobby can leave the customers frustrated after waiting for you to produce their product within a specific time. You could lose customers and end up with negative reviews, missing repeat business and returning customers.

Characteristics or behaviors that serve you well in a hobby do not transfer so well in an environment where you're now expecting a financial return for the services you provide or for the product that you create. Unlike with a hobby, you do not have all the time in the world to complete the job and above all, you cannot afford to get it wrong. Negative reviews speak louder and are more far reaching than compliments.

Skip the Passion... Find the Need
Quick Check for Understanding:

_____

_____

45

Assess Your Needs Before You Start

What do I need to get started or to grow my business? What do I need now? What do I need 6 to 12 months from now? What do I need three years from now? Some people are already in business and looking for the mountain top experience. Well, let's look ahead and cast the vision ahead. Where are you going? What resources do you need? If you are leading others and work with a team, are you so clear on the vision so that they too will accept the vision and come along with you?

When I talk about the vision or resources required for now and over the first six months, that is the short-term. Then, if I talk about the 6 months to 12 months, that's the medium-term, and any reference to three years plus is long-term. With any business, start with the long-term in mind. Lock yourself into being in business three to five years or more so you can look into the long-term success of the business.

I have so many examples of failed attempts. I bought and sold women's fashion and travelled to different places buying beautiful pieces of clothing items. Then I would send messages to all of my friends and on the first Saturday of the month, I would have a group of women from different areas come together. I set up the clothing, and they showed up to buy clothes.

Initially, there was a lot of excitement around it. They selected pieces in the beginning, but it was not a long-term business because I was competing with the retail market, who randomly had sales at any given time. I did not consider that my customer base was mostly my friends and family, so after one or two attempts of coming in to buy something, they were already familiar with my merchandise and the inventory had not changed. They had seen it already and were no longer interested. I didn't anticipate the wear and tear of people coming in to try different clothing all the time and wastage that occurred.

So, consider all of those things as you're thinking through your business plan. There are times when people don't want to create a business plan, but do your due diligence. Sometimes people don't think doing a business plan matters, and the thought of even starting a business plan seems overwhelming.

However, I urge you to consider it differently. Think of it this way: Why is business planning important for my business? This helps you to create a model that you will use in executing your plans. As you go through the exercise, here are some of my thought processes in being accountable and counting the true cost of doing business.

- Am I selling products or services?

- Do I know who or which groups of people I want to make the service or product available to?

- What is the method and process I will use to make sure they know about my products or my services?

- Have I understood the cost to me so I know I am charging accurately, so I can be profitable?

- Are there any other costs (other vendors or suppliers) I must account for?

- What will be my profits (gross/net), and what are my margins?

- What system will I create to automate my business, so every customer has the same experience time and time again?

In your own way, make it as simple as possible to remove all the barriers in your mind that would stop you from attempting to move forward.

Assess Your Needs Before You Start
Quick Check for Understanding:

Model of 10 Business Analysis Tool

When I started the journey of creating a nursing agency, I decided to review ten businesses, and I've always used the model of ten as my process of analyzing where I am operationally and due diligence on a regular basis. I look at small businesses up to the big businesses. I ask, "What do they have? How long have they been in the market? Why are they ranked the way they are? What can I learn from them? What can I discover from the competition? What is their quality rating?

How are they portrayed in the marketplace? How do people perceive them?"

One of the reasons I review ten competitive businesses is so I know where to position my business in that market. I went around the geographical area closest to our possible location, which I would be providing personnel. I desired to be within that environment to see what other businesses were doing and how well they were performing.

Instead of the research information approach, I observed various support groups available to access the research. You can use the internet now. Some information isn't readily available. There are so many now to expand and be more specific with the data. I wish we had as much information then when I started as we do now. You may gather the information from internet browsing, support groups, chambers of commerce, and national statistics data.

Competitive Budget Analysis Template (See in Action Steps)

1. **Selection:** Choose ten businesses (ranging from small to large) in your sector or related to your intended business venture.

2. **General Information:** For each business, fill out:

    a. Business Name:

    b. Years in the Market:

    c. Geographical Location:

3. **Key Questions:** For each of the 10 businesses, answer the following:

    a. Products/Services Offered: What do they have?

b. Market Ranking: Why are they ranked the way that they are?

c. Learning Points: What can I learn from them?

d. Competition Insights: What can I discover about the competition from this business?

e. Quality Rating (1-5):

f. Market Perception: How are they portrayed in the marketplace? How do people perceive them?

4. **Personal Observations:** Visit the geographical area around each business or review websites for on-line businesses and take notes.

a. Operational Insights: What seems to be working for them?

b. Performance Indicators: How well are they performing in the real world?

c. Special Observations: Is anything unique or different about the business that caught your attention?

5. **Positioning:** After reviewing all ten businesses, answer:

a. Positioning Strategy: Based on the analysis, where should you position your business in the market?

b. Unique Selling Proposition (USP): What makes your business stand out?

Comparative Business Analysis
Quick Check for Understanding:

How Big Is Your Market?

How do you substantiate your market? You substantiate your market by identifying the business type. If you're a stylist, what is your location? What are the number of households within that area?

That will tell you the potential target customers. The number of customers that would be within that business. The average income of the community. All this information is available from the national statistics and database organizations. What is the frequency of appointments that you anticipate? What are the number of services you're going to offer? What are the average number of services requested by your customer? When you visit a restaurant, they have so many items on the list. Yes, it's good to have a variety; however, as a start-up, begin with things you know are guaranteed and best-sellers to focus on.

How Big Is Your Market?
Quick Check for Understanding:

_____

_____

_____

Assess the Risks

It's important to assess the risks in starting your business. The risk of starting a business is the cost of time, resources, and inventory. Also, do you need to buy inventory of products as a store owner before generating any income? What do I need to have in-stock to receive a return?

I remember when I started the care agency staffing businesses, there was a moderate investment needed, so being partners in the business, we decided to equally put in the money required to structure the ownership. The percentage of the ownership reflected the person with the concept had a higher share of the business, but the financial input was the same. However, we agreed because the person who generated the idea owned 1% more shares (total 51% shareholder) and the other person had 49%. A partnership agreement was useful to define the nature of relationship, scope of business, and legalities such as what would happen in the event of a falling out or termination.

Do your due diligence and figure out what is needed to start doing business. How many resources? How much time? What are the skills? What expertise is each person bringing? What are the expectations while you're putting this together?

When we started a nursing agency, I was involved in everything. I oversaw administration, operations, and human resources, as well as acting as an owner, founder, and partner.

As we started getting customers, I would pick up the phone and say, "Hi, I'm Effie. How can I assist you?"

They would reply, "I need a nurse."

I looked through the small team's schedules to see the available times. Then, I responded, "Yes, we have a nurse coming tomorrow." Then, I said, "Her name is Effie."

Next, they asked, "What? That's odd to have two people with the same name in the same company."

I explained, "Yes, I'm actually the nurse coming in."

And they would say, "Why is that?"

I responded, "Because we're a start-up, and we want an opportunity to offer the best service. So, I will be coming to provide the service. I'm training other people to take over for me, and I'll know exactly what you need and what you're looking for."

This eliminated some of the initial costs of setting up, but it required a good level of administration, effective communication, and discipline as well.

Assess the Risk
Quick Check for Understanding:

_____

_____

_____

Risk Management Processes

In all my time navigating the unpredictable waters of entrepreneurship, one thing has remained crystal clear: risks are a constant companion on this journey. But it's how we approach and manage these risks that make all the difference. Here's a closer look at my approach to risk management:

- **Identifying Potential Risks:** Before we can address anything, we need to spot it. Whether this is recognizing market shifts, understanding client needs, or internal operational hiccups, it's vital to keep our eyes and ears open. Over time, I've learned that every industry has unique challenges, and by staying attuned, we can better predict and counteract them.

- **Determining the Level of Risk:** Not all risks carry the same weight. I classify them into three categories:

  - **Immediate Risks:** Those that require urgent attention and can impact the business right away.

  - **Medium Risks:** Potential issues might not be immediate but can manifest in the foreseeable future.

  - **Long-term Risks:** These are the ones that lurk in the shadows, possibly affecting the business in the distant future.

- **Risk Resolution Strategy:** Once we've identified and categorized the risks, the next step is crafting a game plan. How do we tackle these challenges? What resources do we need? Who needs to be in the loop? It's all about taking proactive measures, rather than just reacting.

- **Reviewing Risk Resolution:** After implementing our strategies, it's time for reflection. What worked? What didn't? By periodically reviewing our risk resolutions, we can fine-tune our approach and be better prepared for future challenges.

- **Plan of Correction & Business Continuity Strategy:** Mistakes will happen; that's just part of the game. But what's essential is how we respond. Whenever a risk becomes a reality, it's crucial to have a plan of correction in place. This is coupled with a business continuity strategy, ensuring no matter what, we keep moving forward, learning, and growing.

In essence, risk management isn't about avoiding risks—it's about understanding them, embracing them, and turning them into opportunities for growth. There's a famous quote by Vivian Greene that comes to mind which says, "Life isn't about waiting for the storm to pass, it's about learning how to dance in the rain."

Risk Management
Quick Check for Understanding:

Do Your Due Diligence

How do you create a viable business? How many ideas do you have in a day? How many ideas do you have at any given time? There is a due diligence process that is critical to making sure the plan you pursue is viable enough to generate a profitable return. What makes the difference between a good idea to a great business is the due diligence process. I will talk you through this. Most people with an established business would say due diligence is done when you are trying to get an investor, or when you plan to sell your business, or you are bringing in a partner. However, I believe it's the reverse. I do my due diligence as part of laying the foundation, and this forms an integral part of how I build up my own business.

Possibly at some point in the future, someone will be interested in your business because you've done such a great job. Interested parties will say, "We want to be a part of what you have built." Viable businesses create interest and intrigue possible investors and employees as well. This includes anyone you conduct business with. At any given time, the due diligence process is so important in assuring you have taken the time to lay a solid foundation.

I keep coming back to the importance of laying a solid foundation. Ask yourself some important questions: What are the skills I need? Do I need to have a team? What are the different elements that are important as I start? Your business checklist is an important part of creating a viable business plan. This prepares you for the future. This also gives you a place to organize and make sure that you have all the elements in place for your success.

Do Your Due Diligence
Quick Check for Understanding:

Product & Services

Looking at products or services, research the cost of your raw materials. What's the process you need to get the source to your customers? What are the costs that you will incur? (That's specific to products.) If it's a service, what are the terms of engagement? What are the rules of engagement? What is the service type that you're specializing in? Is there any other third-party involved? What are those relationships like? Are there supplier agreements in place? All of these things are important to the initial legal framework.

I have built or invested in businesses in both the product and services sectors. Whether it's sourcing palm oil from West Africa for a skincare line, or staffing care homes, I have always emphasized the need to thoroughly understand every aspect of one's product or service offering. The 7-Figure Business isn't just about having a good idea; it's about executing that idea flawlessly.

For Products:

- **Raw Material Analysis:** One of the first things to tackle is the cost of your raw materials. Where are they coming from? Are there alternative suppliers? Are you getting the best quality for the price? These questions help ensure profitability and sustainability.

- **From Source to Customer:** Understanding the journey of your product from its origin to the end consumer is essential. How is the product manufactured, packaged, stored, and delivered? Each step adds cost and potential challenges.

- **Hidden Costs:** Apart from obvious costs, are there any hidden expenses? This could be in the form of storage, waste management, or even periodic maintenance. Always keep a buffer in your financial planning to cover these unforeseen expenses.

For Services:

- **Terms of Engagement:** When offering a service, clarity is paramount. What are you promising your clients, and in return, what are you expecting? Draft clear service agreements that outline responsibilities, deliverables, and timelines.

- **Rules of Engagement:** This is the guiding principle of how you interact with your clients. It covers everything from communication protocols to dispute-resolution mechanisms.

- **Service Specialization:** Be clear about your niche. In which particular service area do you excel? Having a specialization can set you apart from competitors and give clients a reason to choose you.

- **Third-Party Involvement:** Sometimes, to deliver a service, you might need to collaborate with another party. What's that relationship like? Is it symbiotic? Ensure that there's a clear understanding and agreement with any third-party entities.

- **Supplier & Partnership Agreements:** Legalities are crucial. Whether it's a partnership, a supplier, or a third-party service provider, having clearly drafted agreements in place is non-negotiable. These documents provide a safety net and clarity for all involved.

So, before offering a product or service, arm yourself with this knowledge. It's these finer details, the meticulous planning and understanding, that often spell the difference between a business that's merely surviving and one that's thriving.

Product & Services
Quick Check for Understanding:

Chapter Four

ACTION STEPS

Apply What You've Learned

Pillars of Success

What part(s) of the foundation do you think you need to work on most?

_____

_____

_____

_____

_____

Planning for Success

1. In your role as CEO/Founder/Owner, how best do you serve your business?

_____

_____

_____

_____

2. What tasks or responsibilities are you doing that are better off with someone else on your team?

_____

_____

_____

_____

3. Identify your style of leadership and remove fear of failure by having robust systems and processes.

4. Collaborate with other organizations/service providers who bring value to your business.

5. Regular business review is core to business continuity and success.

6. Which tasks can you outsource?

_____

_____

_____

7. What are the legal/regulatory/legislative requirements in your business sector?

_____

_____

_____

_____

8. What is your unique business proposition? What is your process for refining and improving continually?

_____

_____

_____

_____

_____

Skip the Passion...

How does "passion" get in the way? What disciplines and behavior(s) need transformation? How do you continuously improve? What changes can you make in your business to generate a better financial return?

_____

_____

_____

_____

_____

_____

_____

_____

What Do I Need to Start?

How do you lock into the long-term success of your business? What due diligence do you need to conduct for your business? What is getting in the way of your success? What are the barriers to your entry and growth?

_____

_____

_____

_____

_____

_____

TIMELINE CHART	
Short-Term *3-6 Months*	
Medium Term *6-12 Months*	
Long-Term *1-3 Years +*	

MODEL OF 10 BUSINESS ANALYSIS TOOL

10 BUSINESSES	GENERAL BUSINESS INFORMATION • Business Name • Years In the Market • Geographical Location	KEY QUESTION: What product/service do they offer? • Market Ranking: *Why are they marked the way they are?* • Learning Points: *What can I learn from them?* • Competition Insights: *What can I discover about the competition from this business?*	PERSONAL OBSERVATION • Operational Insights: *What seems to be working for them?* • Performance Indicators: *How well are they performing in the real world?* • Special Observations: *Is anything unique or different about the business that caught your attention?*	POSITIONING • Positioning Strategy: *Based on the analysis, where should you position your business in the market?* • Unique Selling Proposition (USP): *What makes your business stand out?*

10 BUSINESSES (CONT.)	GENERAL BUSINESS INFORMATION	KEY QUESTION: What product/service do they offer?	PERSONAL OBSERVATION	POSITIONING

How Big Is Your Market?

What is the geographic location? Who is your potential target customer? What are your target markets biggest pain points? How do you plan to be a solution for your target audience? How can you reach these individuals?

_____

_____

_____

_____

_____

Assess the Risks

What is the cost of your time? What is the cost of your resources? What skills are needed? Whose expertise will be used? What are partnership expectations? What are the roles and responsibilities? Have you counted the true start-up costs?

_____

_____

_____

_____

_____

_____

ASSESS MANAGEMENT

Immediate Risks	Resolutions:
Medium Risks	Resolutions:
Long-Term Risks	Resolutions:

Do Your Due Diligence

Write any thoughts about the company formation, corporate governance, insurance and risk management, legal report structure, regulatory and statutory obligations, industry license and permit requirements, business financials, operational systems and processes, auditing and review procedures, and business continuity and contingency planning.

_____

_____

_____

_____

_____

_____

_____

CREATE A DUE DILIGENCE CHECKLIST:

__ Company formation

__ Corporate governance (partnership agreements)

__ Insurance and risk management processes

__ Legal reporting structure

__ Regulatory and statutory obligations

__ Industry licensing and permit requirements

__ Business financials

__ Operational systems and processes

__ Auditing and review procedures

__ Business continuity and contingency planning

Product

Count your costs for raw materials. Count the costs for producing your products. How do you ensure you achieve product consistency every time? How do you delight your customers with your products? Do you have good and viable relationships with your suppliers?

_____

_____

_____

_____

_____

Service

What is the service type? Who do you need to engage in your service offerings? What are the terms and rules of engagement? What service level agreements are needed and for how long? Agree on the formalities before commencing in a work relationship.

_____

_____

_____

_____

_____

Services are intangible. Therefore, how do you measure success and business impact? What methods or systems do you use to continuously improve your business?

_____

_____

_____

_____

_____

_____

_____

Chapter Five

RESEARCH AND PLAN

Milestones

NOW THAT YOU'VE STARTED YOUR JOURNEY OF ARTICULATING YOUR business, how do you know when you have achieved the milestone you set for the first three to six months? How do you know that you've now achieved that milestone for the medium term, and then how do you know that you've achieved the milestone for the long term? What tools do you need to access your business viability? What are the indicators of your performance? How do you measure your success? How do you validate that against other competitors?

Determine how big your market is. Let's focus on the healthcare industry for now. It's a billion-dollar market, so when I did my research, I wondered, Can I have a piece of that? Absolutely! I narrowed down where to start. As I understood the size of the market, I learned the potential for me to grow and in what capacity.

We started the business in the United States with one focus. As we rolled out year one, we realized our focus had to be revisited because of the number of similar businesses already occupying space in that area. Businesses were already successful in this industry, so we had to make some adjustments. Always be mindful of what's going on in the industry.

Most businesses are "good" at evaluating themselves, saying how great they are and always having that marketing mindset to sell, sell, sell products, but very few small businesses have an understanding of the importance of listening to what's going on outside.

What are the demands outside of your four walls? How do you add value? What is it that you're providing the solution for in your sector and in your space? Now that you've determined what business you're going to start and have assessed the market and the opportunity, what do you have in your hands? I always ask, "What do you have in your hands?" This is the knowledge of what service or product you can provide. What you have in your hands are the resources available to you as you start on the journey. What you have in your hands is also the faith you will succeed in whatever you set out to achieve.

Milestones
Quick Check for Understanding:

_____

_____

_____

How to Enter a Saturated Market

How do you occupy or get entrance into a market that is saturated? When you are a start-up and there are businesses already established, how do you get in? Here's an example of how I did it.

I remember I went and knocked on doors—literally knocked on numerous doors—and said, "This is who I am, and I happened to be in the area. Here is my marketing information. Will you consider us?" And I can tell you, most of the responses were, "Oh, thank you. We're not interested at the moment. We have suppliers already who are providing your service, so we don't need you." I replied, "Oh, please hold on to that, and I will follow up."

Part of my follow-up process was simply to check in. I didn't have much of a budget, so I kept a spreadsheet and documents to record contacts and progress made. I called to follow up, and as I spoke with a person repetitively, it got to the point that they even laughed when they heard my voice on the phone. That didn't stop me because I knew I had a good service and I wanted to make it available to them. Finally, I got a phone call back from one of those organizations I had been calling regularly, and the individual said, "Hey, you keep telling us that you want to be part of supporting us. I have something that none of my other providers have been able to solve." They needed support with a swimming wellness program, but none of the bigger suppliers were able to provide that service because it was "menial" to them. I responded, "Sure, let me work on that, and I'll get back with you."

I spoke with my team by doing a risk assessment, and we discovered a solution. Then, I replied, "I'm going to supply you with two people so that there's an extra level of support while the patient is in the water, and the patient can benefit from having that comfort of being safe while doing that activity. This will enhance the quality of their life." The client was blown away by my response. He said, "You're going to give me two people, but I've only paid for one. You invested in my success, and you invested in the well-being of the patient that I'm responsible for, and for that reason, I'm going to let you do another piece of support." That client account grew to over 7-figures per annum in revenue.

So, what is it you can do? How can you actually do something different to access a market that's already saturated? Think outside of the box and do something different within your industry.

How to Enter a Saturated Market
Quick Check for Understanding:

_____

_____

_____

Difference Between Marketing & Sales

The best way of defining marketing and sales is the ability to use market research of an industry and turn it into cash. If I understand there is a need within the industry that I want to occupy and I can articulate that need, it means that any interaction or any dialogue I have with a perspective customer will address the problem by providing a solution. Therefore, market research is important in understanding the deficit. It is critical to identify what the problem is, and then tailor a product or service by creating a solution through your business.

Imagine you're a storyteller preparing for a grand performance in a distant village.

Marketing is your understanding of the village's tastes, culture, and traditions. Before setting out on your journey, you listen to whispers about the kinds of stories villagers love and their deepest fears and joys. This is akin to market research in the business world, a deep dive into understanding an industry's unique needs and deficits. You craft a tale tailored for them, weaving in elements that resonate with their unique experiences. This story, or your product or service in the world of commerce, is designed to address a specific need or problem you've identified. It's not just about the story itself, but also about the atmosphere you create: the musical instruments you choose, the backdrop for your performance, and how you'll deliver your tale.

Sales, in contrast, is the night of the performance. As the villagers gather around, you engage them directly with your narrative. You ensure they are engrossed, they feel a part of the story, and by the end, they are moved by it. This direct engagement mirrors your dialogue with potential customers, where the aim is to articulate their needs and provide them with a solution. The applause, the appreciation, and the coins they offer for your tale represent the direct exchange, the culmination of your effort, turning your understanding (market research) directly into value (cash).

In sum, while marketing gives you the insights to craft a solution tailored to industry needs, sales is the art of bringing this solution to your potential customers, addressing their problems, and turning this interaction into tangible success. Both stages are crucial in the quest to make your business story a celebrated one.

Difference Between Marketing and Sales
Quick Check for Understanding:

_____

_____

_____

What Is the SWOT and Why Does It Matter?

One of the pillars of business foundation is the ability to continuously review by conducting a SWOT analysis. That's where you analyze your Strengths,

Weaknesses, Opportunities, and Threats. This is important because it influences your decision making in the business as directed by internal and external forces.

You can extend that even further so there is another form of analysis which goes deeper whereby you analyze the Political, Environment, Social, Technological, Legal, and Economic aspects of where you're operating your business. This is called the PESTEL analysis.

In business, we cannot ignore all of these things. If you are in a place where there is a change in the political environment., it can affect statutory requirements. If a new law is enacted and you aren't aware of it, your business model can be negatively impacted because of a previous law. This change may affect how your business operates or even your ability to do business.

I remember when at one point in one business, our tax rates changed significantly, and that affected the bottom line. If you have not arranged for the correct level of margins or markups within the business and suddenly the cost of supplies increases and the owner hasn't prepared well, this can create problems. Therefore, stay in touch with the factors that influence your business, which are political, economic, social, technological, environmental, and legal. It is important to stay on top of weaknesses, opportunities, and threats. You cannot ignore the impact of these areas for the good of your business.

SWOT and Why It Matters
Quick Check for Understanding:

Legal Structure

The legal structure is important. Registration is necessary for all businesses. So, are you starting as a sole proprietor or formal corporation? What tax applications and different and unique qualifiers are needed? What tax identification do you need to get started as a business? Many businesses require certifications and insurance for public or professional liabilities, so you must have insurance in place. Make sure you find out anything that pertains to your service or industry to operate a legitimate business

Find out what is actually needed. If you're in the food preparation business, what health and safety or food and hygiene licenses or permits do you need before you even get started?

Who are the authorities that regulate your service or industry? Discover assistance through a regulatory agency or advisory group that will help you outline from start to finish. They are vested in your success. I think most people misunderstand the role of a regulator or advisory council. It's in the interest of any economy to have as many start-ups as possible for you to succeed. There are an army of people and resources available to aid you in your success.

Once you have researched the certifications, insurance, tax application, and permits needed for your venture, determine the name of your business. Your name is important. What are the implications of a name? Does it relate to the product? Is it relevant to what you're doing? Can people easily remember that name?

Think of the long term, so as you start your business, naming your business is critical. There is power in the name and even strength in the name. In some industries, this is critical. Where your name sits can also be a hindrance on an alphabetical list, so ABC businesses will be seen before Rainbow Medical Services. If you're dealing with a customer base that's motivated only by looking at the A to Z of names, but not so much the information behind, consider the importance of the name. As you do the Business Strategic Plan in an upcoming chapter, consider the different elements of establishing your business as you create your name.

After you have secured a name, open a bank account and appoint a bookkeeper if you have the resources. In the beginning, I started with a very basic spreadsheet and listed things that I did on a daily basis. What was the cost of items I purchased? What were the expenditures? Initially, there were no resources to claim the money back, but I had to log all of the information until we were ready to reimburse these costs. When the income started coming into the business, the bookkeeper knew where to apply the funds and manage the money.

Securing a domain name is a critical step after finalizing your business name. Numerous online domain registrars can help you lock in an address like www.yourbusinessname.com. It's common to find that your first choice of domain name is already in use, so be ready to think outside the box. If the ".com" version is taken, consider alternatives like ".net". However, be cautious of specific domain extensions, such as ".gov" (reserved for government entities) or ".edu" (designated for accredited educational institutions), which have specific regulatory or societal restrictions. To streamline your domain and social media handle search, platforms like namechk.com can check availability across multiple platforms, sparing you potential headaches down the road.

Legal Structure
Quick Check for Understanding:

_____

_____

_____

Financial Structure

One of the tools essential in building the 7-Figure Business is a road map, and within that road map, there's a financial assessment that you can do for yourself. Within that assessment, it measures your risk tolerance. Are you naturally risk averse to taking risks? Are you naturally someone who is comfortable taking risks?

It takes you a step further than that. Yes, you look at your character and your behaviors based on your past, but it then takes you further. Now that you're putting together a business that you plan to grow over a long term, what are some of the behaviors you need to address? If you have never been good with administrative duties, you can't say, "Well, I'm just not good at that." If you've never been good at managing your own money, it doesn't go away. Those are things that you have to acknowledge. The biggest step to anyone's successes is acknowledging where you have issues or where you have failings, or where you have areas for improvement.

The beauty of this is once you've acknowledged that, you step out and identify people that complement this area or who are stronger in that way. You can either employ or enter into a partnership or connect with an expert in the industry or use a skilled expert who provides that service and focuses on it. A service that comes to mind is taxes. If you have individuals that specialize in tax law, he or she is aware of your particular industry, make sure you're available to listen and learn from the experts.

Be intentional and participate in many opportunities to learn every day. I listen to webinars and take part in advisory group discussions about things specific to the industries that are important to me.

Make sure that you are assessing your levels of risk tolerance. Be persistent to the daily diligence of business management. Monotonous activities are a part of doing business. If you are complaining about being in a 9 to 5, I can tell you right away it's going to be difficult to start a business, because during the start-up stages a business is all-consuming as you set up your frameworks, systems, and business models.

You can work up to 16 hours a day or more. And within those 16 hours, being a business owner can take place Monday through Sunday. Do you have the stamina to live up to that? Do you have the support within your own family attending to the demands you have on a daily basis to allow you the time to focus? Make sure you have a reality check to ensure you have prepared yourself to succeed.

The financial structure with clear parameters is important. Within the structure, review on a regular basis. This isn't fixed. It's always moving. If there are parts that need to change because you are selling pieces of equipment, and the business who manufactures that item increases their pricing, you need to have a way of evaluating and making the adjustments quickly. Also, communicating with your customer base is important in making them aware of the changes. Some changes can happen at any given time.

Some of my financial assessments have not been perfect, so I can honestly say regardless of failing, I remained committed. I have taken on the opportunity as a learning experience. I am open to critiques, and I avail myself to sitting under the teaching and guidance of experts who are opinion leaders in a specific area of influence for my business.

The financial assessment will help you discover the cost and give you an idea of how much your business will be worth. This can be the reassurance within yourself to confirm the idea of moving forward. This is where you would say, "I want to do this, and I have the process laid out clearly to achieve my goal. In the end, I will accomplish what I set out to do." The financial assessments are important.

As you take action, be dedicated to succeeding, in spite of the challenges that will come. The Future 7-Figure Business Owner must be willing to stay the course and see it through.

Financial Structures
Quick Check for Understanding:

_____

_____

_____

"We" or "I" Teams

My greatest opportunity in starting and building a business was in the understanding that the business concept has never been about me. So, the desire to start a business was to provide a solution within a specific sector/industry. It's solution based, and the solution is not for me, so that understanding must align with the fact that it's not about "me" or "I." It's about "We."

Even if I am an individual sole proprietor in a business, I still have to engage with my customers. If I am working alone from home with other people—third parties—it's never about me. I must value the role of each of those components or individuals or entities. The 7-Figure Business Owner appreciates that together "We" can put together an excellent response, product, or service needed in the space. That is our calling in business, so I've never struggled with appreciating being part of a wider team or a greater team because we have a common vision in mind. I understand that I am privileged to be the one who might come up with that initiative to say let's go this way; however, it's all about teams and not about me.

Creating teams can be such a joy, especially when you have teams that bring value to a specialized area. Therefore, being a part of a team means everyone brings value, so surround yourself with valuable people. If you all have a mutual level of respect for what each party offers, then you're set to do well. Every exceptional business has an element of collaboration, so choose well based on the assessment of how each party will contribute to the team.

If this is a partnership, there are different types of partnerships, which include financial, intellectual knowledge based, and service specific partnerships. This is when I need to produce a particular item, so I collaborate with someone who can give me the required product through this collaboration. If I'm collaborating with someone and it's just for one specific project, I'm very clear from the beginning. There is no expectation raised beyond that one project. If that works well, we may decide to move on to other projects. However, we will sit down and review the next stage of the relationship.

One of the dangers of start-ups is the immature or premature expectation of what each person is bringing because there hasn't been effective communication of each person's role, responsibilities, and what they bring to the table. Therefore, make expectations clear so no misunderstandings or reading between the lines confuse participants. Sometimes, this can be uncomfortable. However, state exactly what we're going to create and what we expect to get out of this. These are the roles, responsibilities, and expectations of each party. They may state their expectations of me or the business owner, so you have the understanding from the start. It actually makes collaboration more fruitful as you move toward the end goal. "It's not about me... it's never about me."

"We" or "I" Teams
Quick Check for Understanding:

_____

_____

_____

Partnerships

Partnerships allow you to offer a better service, so collaborating can strengthen your offering by developing a business synergy with other individuals or companies. A number of organizations can come together, each being strong in their own area of expertise between those collaborative organizations. You can create a solution that is impactful on a global scale. Whereas if you did it all by yourself, you are limited to the time and space that you occupy, so there's a strength from each partner within a collaboration.

Responsibilities and roles are shared, so it takes away that risk of *Oh, goodness, I'm exposed. I'm not sure what to do.* You have a safe place to flush out the ideas and test what you're trying to do. Over the years. I've come to appreciate it's not being 100% business owner that quantifies your level of success or level of return. I've learned to understand I would rather be a part of something great while having a smaller stake than being at the risk of becoming extinct because I can't stay up to date with the demands of the market, service, or needs of my customers. Consider the benefits carefully as you collaborate and create partnerships.

Partnerships
Quick Check for Understanding:

_____

_____

_____

Chapter Five

ACTION STEPS

Apply What You've Learned

Milestones

What are your business milestones? Make sure to be as detailed as possible, this will create the overall vision for your business.

Short term (3–6 months)

_____

_____

_____

Medium term (6–12 months)

_____

_____

_____

Long-term (1–3 years)

_____

_____

_____

How do you know when you have achieved your milestone? What tools do you need to assess your business viability? What performance measures or indicators have you put in place? What are your measures of success? How do you validate your performance against your competitors?

_____

_____

_____

_____

_____

How to Enter a Saturated Market?

How much market share do you look to acquire? What specialist opportunities exist for you? What are your areas of focus (immediate, medium, long-term)? Think over your areas for growth.

_____

_____

_____

_____

_____

Market Demands Versus Your Own Business Perception

What is the problem? How have you identified the opportunity to solve the problem? What do you have in your hands as a solution to the problems identified?

_____

_____

_____

_____

_____

_____

Marketing Strategy

What is your marketing strategy that will differentiate you from established competitors? How will you stand out and above the crowds? What lasting impression will you make? What is your value proposition that will bring value for your customers? What can you do differently to get access into a saturated market? What does "thinking outside of the box" mean in your business?

_____

_____

_____

_____

_____

_____

_____

_____

_____

_____

_____

_____

Identify a problem (need) in the market that, when articulated and implemented well and consistently, results in your business creates business solutions that generate income (financial return and value). Use market research to identify the deficit and problem to lead to the solutions for a viable business solution.

_____

_____

_____

_____

_____

_____

_____

One of the pillars of business foundation is the ability to continually review the business by conducting a SWOT analysis: Strengths, Weaknesses, Opportunities, and Threats. What influences the decision making in your business? Conduct the PESTEL analysis: Political, Economic, Social, Technological, Environmental, and Legal.

SWOT ANALYSIS	
Strengths	**Weaknesses**
Opportunities	**Threats**

PESTEL Analysis

POLITICS	ECONOMICAL	SOCIAL	TECHNOLOGICAL	ENVIRONMENTAL	LEGAL

Legal Structure

What is the business formation structure? What tax identification and registrations are required? What licenses and/or permits do you need? What protection and business insurance do you require? What regulatory requirements must your business comply with? What services do you need to get started (finance, bookkeeping, and HR)? What is the relevance of your business name? Does it relate to the products or services provided? Is it relevant to what you are doing? Can people remember your business name?

_____

_____

_____

_____

_____

_____

"We" not "I" Team

Being in business is always about providing solutions to problems. Align with the posture of "We" not "me," even as a sole proprietor. There is always a need to engage with others as stakeholders to your business. Appreciate being part of a greater and wider team. It's all about TEAM and not about me. How will you implement the concept of having a team?

_____

_____

_____

_____

_____

_____

_____

_____

_____

_____

TEAM makes the dream work. Every member of the team brings value. Every good and exceptional business has an element of collaboration. How and who adds value to your business idea or concept?

_____

_____

_____

_____

_____

_____

_____

Partnerships

Types of partnerships: What type of partners do you need? Intellectual (knowledge based), Financial (investor based) and/or Service specific (expertise in specific service provision, i.e., graphic designer)?

_____

_____

_____

_____

_____

_____

Strong Collaborations

Clarify the reason and context of collaboration: roles, responsibilities, and timeframe for collaboration. Not all collaborations are permanent.

_____

_____

_____

_____

_____

_____

Identify benefits for specific partnerships. How does this partnership allow you to offer a better service? How does this partnership create a global solution? Is this partnership beneficial for all parties? Does this partnership create a safe place to explore greater possibilities?

_____

_____

_____

_____

_____

_____

_____

What are your 3 take-aways from chapter 5?

1. _____

_____

_____

_____

2. _____

_____

_____

_____

3. _____

_____

_____

_____

Chapter Six

FINANCIAL REPORTS

As much as you can simplify the financial planning, this is the same as your personal budget. You know on a typical day or on a monthly basis the cost of your rent and living expenses, so you base the budget of your income using the same simple principles. However, you apply it to business.

My first business was in my daughter's bedroom in our home because I tried to reduce the level of cost by planning well. The downstairs living room was the place that I would use as the reception area. The upstairs bedroom was my daughter's room and the office. As people came, my mom would serve them tea, so don't have this idea of spending a great deal of money by opening a big store with all these expenses.

Make sure you are compliant with the regulations for legal operations within the guidelines of your business sector. When I started, I would have licensing inspectors come to my home to make sure that I worked to the expected regulations. I adhered to the expected operating policies and procedures required for us to occupy that space.

Starting in a place where you can control costs is crucial, and it's important not to make any assumptions along the way. Recording and counting everything is a best practice. What are some financial reports that are crucial at any given time? I always say there are four, including the first one, which is the budget and projections. Once

I know what my budget is, I know what I'm working towards. Therefore, after planning my budget, I create a budget for more than a year at a time, initially starting with 3 to 6 months and then moving on to months 6 to 12. This helps with planning. What is the budget? What am I projecting in terms of expenditures for the year?

Financial reports are very important to your business, as well as the **budgeting and projection, balance sheet, cash flow statement**, and **profit and loss statement**.

Budget and Projections

INCOME STATEMENT

Particulars	Assumptions	Year 1	Year 2	Year 3	Year 4	Year 5
Revenue		40,000	75,000	100,000	200,000	300,000
Gross margin%		55%	55%	55%	55%	55%
Cost sales		18,000	33,750	45,000	90,000	135,000
Gross margin		22,000	41,250	55,000	110,000	165,000
R&D expenses		5,000	6,000	8,000	17,000	25,000
Selling expenses		6,000	7,000	8,000	16,000	24,000
General and administrative		5,000	6,000	9,000	17,000	26,000
Operating expenses		16,000	19,000	25,000	50,000	75,000
Depreciation	20%	5,000	14,000	11,600	9,680	11,744
Operating income		1,000	8,250	18,400	50,320	78,256
Finance costs	4.00%	600	2,248	1,615	956	487
Income before tax		400	6002	16,785	49,364	77,769
Income tax expense	20%	80	1,200	3,357	9,873	15,554
Net income		320	4,802	13,428	39,491	62,215

The **profit and loss statement** helps a business owner keep account of all their income and costs of the company. It helps compare the forecast against actual income, so the profit and loss help you to keep account of all the company costs. This assists you in forecasting the income against expenditures.

PROFIT AND LOSS STATEMENT

	September 24, 2023	September 25, 2022	September 26, 2021
Net Sales			
Products	316,199	297,392	220,747
Services	78,129	68,425	53,768
Total net sales	394,328	365,817	274,515
Cost of Sales			
Products	201, 471	192,266	151,286
Services	22,075	20,715	18,273
Total cost of sales	223,546	212,981	169,559
Gross margin	170,782	152,836	104,956
Operating Expenses			
Research and development	26,251	21,914	18,752
Selling, general and administrative	25,094	21,973	19,916
Total operating expenses	51,345	43,887	38,668
Operating Income	119,437	108,949	66,288
Other income /(expense) net	-334	258	803
Income before provision for income taxes	119,103	109,207	67,091
Provision for income taxes	19,300	14,527	9,680
Net Income	99,803	94,680	57,411
Earnings Per Share:			
Basic	6.15	5.67	3.31
Diluted	6.11	5.61	3.28
Shares used in computing earnings per share:			
Basic	16,701,271	16,215,963	17,352,119
Diluted	16,325,819	16,864,919	17,528,214

The **balance sheet** is everything that your business owns, which are the assets, what is owed, and the liabilities. (See example on the next page.)

BALANCE SHEET

ASSETS	
CASH	
Checking Account	$5,000
Savings Accounts	
CDs (Certificates of Deposit)	
Other Cash	
TOTAL CASH	**$5,000**
INVESTMENTS	
Life Insurance (Cash Surrender Value)	
Brokerage Account (Non-Retirement)	
Securities (Stocks, Bonds, Mutual Funds)	
Investment Real Estate (Market Value)	
Treasury Bills/Notes	
Other Investments	
TOTAL INVESTMENTS	
PROPERTY	
Primary Property (Market Value)	$200,000
Automobiles (Present Value)	
Bullion (Silver, Gold, Etc.)	
Jewelry, Art, and Collectibles	
Other Property	
TOTAL PROPERTY	**$200,000**
RETIREMENT	
Retirement Account (IRA, 401K)	$20,000
Pension and Project Sharing	
Social Security ($ Month *240)	
Other Assets	
TOTAL RETIREMENT	**$20,000**
NOTES & ACCOUNTS RECEIVABLE	
Notes and Accounts Receivable	
Other Notes	
TOTAL NOTES	
TOTAL ASSETS	**$225,000**

LIABILITIES	
Mortgage on Real Estate	
Mortgages on Investment Real Estate	
Credit Accounts, Bills Due, Etc.	$1,000
Accounts Payable	
Loans on Life Insurance	
Loans on Profit Sharing/Pension	
Loans of Retirement Accounts	
Unpaid Taxes (Current Year)	
Other Liabilities	
TOTAL LIABILITIES	**$1,000**
NET WORTH (ASSETS/LIABILITIES)	**$224,000**

The **cash flow statement** shows the cash coming in and out of the business over a period. If you're doing a cash flow, you can do it for a year at a time. This gives you the fullness of understanding of the cash requirements at each stage of the business.

CASH FLOW STATEMENT

OPERATING ACTIVITIES

Sales Receipts	$50,000,000
Payments for Products	($25,000,000)
Payments for Operations	($20,000,000)
Interest Payments	($1,000,000)
Taxes	($2,270,500)
Extraordinary Items	$2,000,000
NET CASH FLOW FROM OPERATING ACTIVITIES	**$3,729,500**

INVESTING ACTIVITIES

Purchase of New Fixed Assets (Property/Machinery)	($21,000,000)
Interest Received	$50,000
NET CASH FLOW FROM INVESTING ACTIVITIES	**($20,950,000)**

FINANCING ACTIVITIES

Short-term Debt	$7,000,000
Long-term Debt	$11,000,000
New Equity Issued	$5,000,000
NET CASH FLOW FROM FINANCING ACTIVITIES	**$23,000,000**

CASH FLOW

Cash at the Beginning of the Year	$1,000,000
Cash at the End of the Year	$7,220,500
NET INCREASE (DECREASE IN CASH)	**$6,220,500**

Financial reports play a critical role in managing your business. It enables you to compare your forecasted income against the actual income, so you can keep track of all the company costs. This helps you in predicting the actual income against expenditures. If you are doing a cash flow analysis, you can do it for a year at a time. This will provide you with a better understanding of the cash requirements at each stage of your business.

Partnerships
Quick Check for Understanding:

_____

_____

_____

Refining Your Model

Now we will look at the finance model. This model demands that you forecast for a good and viable profitable business for your future. How do you forecast your income well? You must know the size of the market.

If you're looking to start a business as a hair stylist in a certain area, it's important to first understand the demographics of that area. For example, if you're planning to offer styling services to women above a certain age in a particular location, you need to analyze the foot traffic in that area as well as the number of competitors. Conducting thorough research will help you to determine the most popular styles people desire, and you can price your services accordingly. By knowing the size of the market and the costs involved, you can make your business financially sustainable and simplify your financial projections. This way, you can predict the forecast return on your investment.

Is the income seasonal? Is the income higher at certain times of the year than others? How will the owner reduce the cost during that time? Think of all those things in the financial planning. Is the business cyclical? I know with some farming, they do rotational crop farming, where each season is based on the climate. They will have a certain crop, and then they will rotate. There are different benefits for doing that. I'm not a farmer by nature or training, but I am aware of the process and the way they structure. Someone could have a salad bar, which is great in the summer, but what do you do in the winter? Are you going to do a soup bar as well? So, whatever it is that you're doing, plan the year ahead.

There is a season when the temporary staffing agency sector is difficult because of children being out of school on holidays or because they must attend their family events. During this time, it's hard to get people to come to work. No one is looking after the children over the summer break, so build all those things into a model of operation earmarked or flagged with some of the challenges coming ahead. Is your business scalable? Can you take on an employee for a full-time basis and another temporary? Use minimal resources initially. Then add on as needed.

Refining Your Model
Quick Check for Understanding:

_____

_____

_____

Markup Versus Profit Margin

Understanding the difference between markup and profit margin is crucial for any business.

- **What is Profit Margin?** It represents the revenue remaining after the cost of goods is subtracted.

- **What is Markup?** Markup is the difference between the retail price of the product and its original purchasing cost.

Many businesses struggle because they don't grasp these concepts. Building a knowledgeable team that holds each other accountable can be the key to success. As an owner, self-accountability is equally important.

Markup Versus Profit Margin
Quick Check for Understanding:

_____

_____

_____

The Importance of Accountability in Business

Every entrepreneur faces days of feeling overwhelmed or discouraged. Challenges, both personal and business-related, are inevitable. It's crucial to:

- Have accountability partners both personally and in business.

- Regularly check in to ensure everyone remains accountable for their responsibilities.

Importance of Accountability in Business
Quick Check for Understanding:

_____

_____

_____

Doing Business Globally: Key Considerations

Venturing into global markets presents unique challenges:

- **Time Zones:** Different active hours can impact coordination.

- **Currency:** Fluctuating exchange rates can affect profitability.

- **Shipping:** Ensure your account for shipping costs and delivery expectations.

- **Delivery Time:** International distribution often takes longer.

When you are doing your financial planning, always account for these variables to ensure smooth operations and sustained profitability.

Doing Business Globally
Quick Check for Understanding:

_____

_____

_____

Operations

The organizational structure is important for any organization. Many people get afraid when you talk about organizational structures. I actually like it because this helps solidify and clarify the roles and responsibilities. An organization's structure is supposed to reflect the type of service you're providing and the level of management, support, operational aspects, and components of that organization as part of your growth strategy, which also include the roles needed at various points. You may need to bring in additional resources, so you may have different types of organograms or organizational charts as a visual because they help you identify who you need and their roles.

The organizational structure is important because this:

- Creates clarity of the structure

- Creates clarity in roles and responsibilities

- Is effective as an organization evaluation tool

- Is visually effective in identifying who is needed, the role to be filled, and the right reporting lines

Operation
Quick Check for Understanding:

_____

_____

_____

Clarity of Roles and Responsibilities

Effective planning and coordination of priorities play a crucial role in the success of a start-up. Let me explain how this works. Once you have created a forecast and budget, you will have a clear idea of the costs involved and can scale up your business accordingly. Start with yourself and a minimum number of support staff. Then, as your business grows, you will be able to determine at which point of growth you need to go to the next level of planning. Therefore, good coordination and planning should be your topmost priority.

Looking back, I realize if I had known the importance of good planning from the outset, I could have saved a lot of time. Although the time I spent writing policies and procedures was beneficial, it would have been easier if I had worked with an expert who could have created policies, procedures, and kept up to date with the changing laws in my industry. I now understand that planning ahead is the best use of time for any business owner.

I could have spent more time doing and growing the business functions. Also, using the legal organization allowed me to stay up to date with the changes in legislation. It allowed my business to comply with the various regulatory requirements. Outsourcing freed me up to focus on the business strategy and the growth of the business so you should consider outsourcing some of the services.

I remember early on outsourcing the payroll functions and the finance reporting until we grew enough to justify employing someone on a full-time basis to bring in house. The bookkeeping, accounting, and human resource functions can be outsourced. It means finding someone who's qualified to know exactly what the law requires you to do and to comply with as a business. This person is responsible for making sure you've taken care of the money in a legal manner and how much you want to progress in growing your business. People can set the most modest or conservative targets as they want to, and there are others who set the most outlandish and exorbitant targets.

Realistic goals are based on your understanding of the market, the ability to do your due diligence, and your willingness to do each step. Business implementation of step-by-step processes and continuous reviews leads to success. One of the things regarding financial planning in the beginning of my entrepreneurial journey was I didn't build enough into the start-up cost. I should have created a buffer since I was not making money from day one. Make sure you've built that into the plan if you have a business that won't make money from day one. This should be in your budgeting and forecasting.

Clarity of Role and Responsibility
Quick Check for Understanding:

_____

_____

_____

Effective Planning and Coordination for Start-up Success

Proper planning and prioritizing are vital for the success of start-ups. Here's why:

Resource Allocation: It's essential to evaluate the resources required for the short-term, medium-term, and long-term phases of your business. This ensures steady growth without overstretching.

Solid Foundations: Clear planning pinpoints what's essential, helping you establish a firm foundation for your business from the outset.

Outsourcing Benefits: Delegating specific business functions, like staying updated with legislation, regulatory requirements, or bookkeeping, can be advantageous. This allows you to focus on your core competencies while ensuring compliance and efficiency.

Setting Targets: Ground your goals in reality by setting targets based on a thorough understanding of your market. Realistic expectations pave the way for sustainable growth.

Key Performance Measures

Key performance measures or indicators around financial planning can answer questions like:

- How much money and resources do you need to get started before you can make money?

- How many resources do you need before you can generate a financial return?

- What is your ability to create customers as a business before you see a return?

One of the errors or oversights I experienced in another business was I used the model that had worked successfully in one market and thought it would be replicated in a new market. As much as I had the same product and service in the two markets, the process of getting to market or the actual launch of the business took far longer in another market. I had not anticipated that, so there was a knowledge gap in understanding the regulations, which were significantly different. Therefore, this meant there was a greater cost from one market to another.

Make sure you are prepared for some of those things you could take for granted. Don't say I've done this for so long, and I know what to do. If you're selling in the beauty industry or you're in the food manufacturing space, you've been doing it on a small scale already, but are your ingredients available for the long term? When you have to scale up for tens of thousands or hundreds of thousands of orders compared to when you were just doing a thousand orders, are you going to offer the same quality product? When you have scaled up your business, are you able to scale and continue to enjoy the benefit of the customer review and feedback saying you're still on top of the game? Are you still giving the greatest service? How do you stay relevant in your business? Who are your brand ambassadors? How do you say yes to an ambassador? Yes, you are your own brand ambassador, but other than yourself, who are they? How do you stay relevant?

Effective Planning and Coordination for Start-Up Success
Quick Check for Understanding:

Always Reviewing

With the pillars of business success and with continuous improvement in mind, track your performance. Always track how well you're doing. We have daily and sometimes weekly meetings, and the objective of those meetings is to review and track the performance. These types of meetings are conducted differently. There could be advisory board level discussions. There are operational meetings, where each individual unit has an understanding of the long-term vision you've set for the business, and you're measuring the performance against those objectives. You're making sure that you're staying on target with the strategy. Stay on point with delivering according to the strategy.

Analyze! Analyze! Analyze! Analyzing your business is crucial. Never hesitate to check and assess if what you're doing is still relevant to your customers and the market. If there is a change in trends, purchasing behavior, or access to different ways of buying, inform your customers that online-based businesses are becoming more important. With the new normal, it is no longer necessary to meet in person, so look for technologies that can help you adapt to this new environment while still providing the same level of service.

With advances in technology, we've seen that coming together to meet in person as a team is no longer a requirement, so come up with the technologies that allow you to adapt in that environment while you still continue to provide the level of quality of business that your customers expect.

When you get it wrong—and you will get it wrong sometimes—put your hand up and say you got it wrong. Then put in place a plan of correction. Take account of the errors you make as a business, own them, and commit yourself to making improvements by taking action. The best way to do this is to have a system that allows you to continuously analyze your performance as a business.

Why is it important to track your performance and analyze? Because if you don't understand the things inside and outside that impact your business, you could end up becoming extinct.

Make sure you are continuously reviewing, improving, and always listening. Most small businesses are so focused on the output and getting the product or service to market, but they lose sight of the environment and changes that can happen.

There are times when a change is so significant or it may appear as a significant change, but if you had paid attention for years along the way, you would have noticed the red flags indicated. Different things can present a challenge for business. There could be a change in legislation, which can impact how you do business. Therefore, always analyze, review, and stay up to date with all those changes because they can impact your business for better or for worse.

How does a change in management assist you? It enables your organization to transition from the "business as usual attitude" to a desired future state of greater productivity, greater efficiencies, more profitability—results. Have someone else give you that review. It doesn't have to be a paid-for service, but there are so many indicators that you can utilize to have a clean and honest review. I call it a "naked in the mirror" experience. You may not like everything you see, but you have to deal with this because it won't change unless you do something.

There are times you can look at yourself in the mirror and you might not like what you see. However, that's who you are, though you may not like to see certain things about your business. There may be things you may need to improve, so you must be able to have that naked in the mirror experience. This is where the business owner reflects on every aspect and looks at where the business is headed. Reflective review is good. Failing to address changes in your PESTEL or SWOT analysis can contribute to the breakdown of your business.

Accept errors or things you may have overlooked in managing your business. There's nothing wrong with making a mistake, but use that as a learning experience. Some of the best learning I have had in my business journey came from experiences that were painful, hurtful, or nerve-racking, but I have used those to strengthen myself and my business. Filing for bankruptcy was earth shattering, and yet it provided the greatest education. As someone told me, "You paid your school fees when you failed. Now use that education and make good."

The foundation of a successful businesses is continuous improvement and development, growing to greater to take advantage of opportunities. Every opportunity presents a blessing. If you're going through a situation that is seemingly difficult, I think it's important to take the emotion out of it and ask yourself, *What am I learning from this?* The times I encountered hurtful experiences, either through negative reviews or people just having a certain way of operating which didn't line up with my own desire, I took a step back and thought, *Okay, what am I learning from this?* And to be honest, there's always something significant to learn.

Also, remember in the success to celebrate the positives as well. Create various ways to give yourself and partners an applause.

Make it your focus to know the areas for improvement in the business. Sometimes this is an area you need to revisit. Some of the things we decide to embark on within the business don't necessarily line up with the original plan and purpose. However, we will move forward anyway, so take all of the critiques and feedback. Use it as a weapon for progress on ongoing and continuous improvement.

Always Reviewing
Quick Check for Understanding:

Chapter Six

ACTION STEPS

Apply What You've Learned

Financial Reports

Forecasting your income means you must know the size of your market, and in order to do so, you must answer the questions below:

- Who are your demographics?

- Where is your market location?

- Who is your target customer?

- Do you know your number of competitors?

- Financial sustainability (short-term/long-term)

- Is the business seasonal/cyclical?

- Which operating model is suited to your business?

- Is your business scalable and can you bring in additional resources when needed rather than as a fixed/permanent cost?

Markup Versus Profit Margin

What affects your ability to do business well internationally?

- Differences in time zones?

- Currency conversions losses and exchange rates?

- Shipping and distribution costs globally?

- Time taken to distribute products internationally?

Accountability

How are you holding yourself accountable? How are you staying accountable within your business? Do you have a team that holds each other accountable?

_____

_____

_____

_____

_____

_____

Organizational Structure

Circle the type of business you plan to create:

Sole Proprietor

Partnership

LLC

Corporation

S-Corporation

Clarity of Roles and Responsibilities

Good planning and coordination of priorities is critical to the success of start-ups: Evaluate resources needed for short-term, medium-term, and long-term. Clarify what is critical in creating a solid foundation. Add roles and responsibilities as needed.

- Outsourcing:

- Bookkeeping:

- Advertising:

- Legislation:

- Technical Systems:

- Administrative Assistant:

- Automation System:

-

-

-

Key Performance Indicator

Financial Planning

1. How much finance do you need to get started?

2. How much resources are required before you can achieve a financial return?

3. What is your ability to create customers before you receive income—financial return—in your business?

4. What are the financial oversights that may hinder your ability to succeed in your business?

5. What are the knowledge gaps that can result in greater start-up costs?

6. What ingredients or products are crucial to your products that may run out or cost more and affect your pricing model?

Staying Relevant In Your Business

- Are you your business ambassador?

- Who are your brand ambassadors?

Always Reviewing

Continuous Improvement

- Are you still on target with your strategy?

- Are you delivering?

- Check, assess, and verify that what you do is relevant to your industry and still meets customer expectations.

- Verify if there are any market changes (trends/purchasing style).

- Is business being done differently?

How You Deal with Business Mistakes Checklist

(Be honest with yourself.)

- ☐ Put your hand up and take ownership when you get it wrong.

- ☐ Accept it when you get it wrong.

- ☐ Put in place an action plan with corrective measures.

- ☐ Take account of errors and mistakes.

- ☐ Repair, improve, correct.

What are your 3 take-aways from chapter 6?

1. _____

_____

_____

_____

2. _____

_____

_____

_____

3. _____

_____

_____

_____

BUILDING WEALTH VERSUS GETTING RICH

BUILDING WEALTH REQUIRES YOU TO HAVE A GOOD UNDERSTANDING OF financial terms and language, even when you rely on a financial expert to guide you. In order to build wealth, you must understand budgeting, projections, forecasting, profit and loss, balance sheets, and all finance management reports. Managing money equates to building wealth, and building wealth equates to long-term business growth. Profitable long-term business growth means building wealth.

Creating Business Value

How do you create value? In so many ways, the greatest value that most people desire is a value of owning their own time. By being a business owner, most will say it's the financial freedom, but there are also other aspects, like the ability to acquire assets or to create intellectual property. If you have something specific to the knowledge base and the ability as the "only" person who knows how to do a specific thing the day when you aren't feeling well, you are restricted in your ability to work, which means that the work stops.

There are so many ways of recreating, reinventing, scaling, or multiplying by being innovative to grow the work beyond yourself. The best way of creating financial freedom is having something that is not only reliant on you. Create a system which implements actions without you facilitating each time.

Business value also links to goodwill. This means the number of repeat customers, the number of customers that become brand ambassadors and refer others to your business.

These are people who will either say good things about you, will endorse your product, or are willing to return and purchase more, so pay attention to your customer service. Pay attention to the pain you are solving and even the reason why you started business. That is the solution, so continue.

Creating Business Value
Quick Check for Understanding:

_____

_____

_____

Making Money Work for You

I am venturing into a new business opportunity. The plan is to manufacture a skincare line. I am aware that I need to understand how to monetize the plan, which distribution channels to use, and the networks required to make this venture successful. This is a new area for me and something I am not accustomed to doing.

Therefore, there has to be a different way of approaching the business plan. There is no one financial road map I can apply across industries. There are certain things that are similar or will be consistent in every plan. However, each plan is different based on the industry, service, or product being provided. Supply chains are also important.

A great example of how businesses are continuously reviewing their financial model is a retail store or a supermarket. During the COVID-19 pandemic, they had to revisit their plan and their business strategy, especially when the lockdown season was at its peak. They turned every supermarket superstore into a distribution center. They had all the inventory in place, but the model changed from having customers come in to buy goods and products to them taking online orders and delivering to customers' homes.

In addition, they retained many employees and created more jobs because they now needed a higher number of staff to implement that level of distribution. Therefore, you must understand your supply, distribution channels, a way of managing the process, and a timeline for having inventory and how to deliver items to customers. At which point do you need to change or adjust?

What does that look like in a tangible sense? How many of the processes do you have in place that can be automated? What's another way of creating efficiencies within your business. If I have an activity, I can use a software to achieve and save information centrally, so everyone who logs in has that information available. It's virtually up to date anytime they're reading it. This means my customers will have a better experience because anyone who they speak with in the team will have access to the same information. So, how do you automate your systems? How do you automate your processes correctly?

Making Money Work for You
Quick Check for Understanding:

_____

_____

_____

Who Is On the Winning Team?

Now that you've decided to build that 7-Figure Business, who is on your winning team? It's important to have the right people on the team as you embark on your journey to being the 7-Figure Business Owner. Your winning team includes an accountant or a bookkeeper. This financial person will assist you in understanding the model for your business and the importance of many transactions, which include identifying the best bank to support your business needs.

Plan from one to five years, so if you're projecting a certain level of growth and you have transactions that need to be done a certain way, make sure you've done your due diligence. Check to ensure the bank you're choosing is the right one for the long term. There is nothing harder than having to change banks halfway through because you don't have the services you need for the type of products you're selling. Keep this in mind.

Marketing is another aspect of the winning team. Are you doing enough to understand the marketplace? Have you done enough research to analyze where you are going to position yourself as you start the business? Most times when we talk about marketing, people automatically think about business development. However, I'm talking about marketing. What information do you have pertaining to the market you will be pitching yourself and where your business will start from? Where do you plan to grow? Is the market available? Is there someone who can be a part of the team that may offer access to the information and time?

When I talk about a winning team, I do not plan to bring everyone in on a full-time basis. It's tapping into the resources with an independent contractor, or a long-term arrangement based on your needs until you can employ the individual full time. You need insurance for your business, so secure the right insurance products for your goods and services. A support network made up of mentors must be a part of the winning team as well. These may be people you do not have a personal relationship with, but they've become leaders in that industry. You can glean from their experiences.

Being in business now compared to being in business almost 20 years ago is such a different experience. Many possible business owners risk being mentally arrested by the level of information available to the point of not even moving forward. Therefore, determine what is adequate information before you proceed. Stay focused.

The greatest member of the winning team is YOU. Many people overlook the value that they bring. Don't ignore your passion. The fact that you've decided to go into business means you have found the strength within yourself to be passionate enough about whatever business venture drives you. So, invest in yourself and take time to identify areas of improvement. If you've created a product or service, continuously improve on the customer experience. Take time to analyze and maximize. Do a self-assessment and be honest with yourself. Have other people critique you and process the information. Take the information in and work from there.

Finally, what is your attitude about money? This is also an important part of the winning team. If you shy away from addressing difficult money decisions, then that's going to be so evident in how your business moves forward. If your attitude to money is motivated by quick fixes, that will also be evident in how your business will roll out. If your attitude is, I'll invest now in the things that need to be done now and enjoy the benefits much later, this is the model most successful business owners engage in for the long term, and there is sustained growth and longevity.

Who Is On the Winning Team?
Quick Check for Understanding:

Do You Have Enough Cash?

Do you have enough finances needed to get started? Be careful not to underestimate start-up expenses. Do not over project the revenue and income in the first year. What could delay you in achieving your set financial targets? Have you accounted for the size of market share that your competitors have within your industry? What is the financial model that you will use as a measuring stick for your business sector? If a business owner doesn't account for the true cost of getting started, he or she can possibly generate losses that aren't accounted for, so plan well.

Do You Have Enough Cash?
Quick Check for Understanding:

What Makes You Money?

What makes you money? I learned from a very early age even before starting a business the best corporate organizations had systems and processes in place. They had efficiencies in how things were done. These organizations continually reviewed roles and responsibilities while continuously refining and improving their processes, policies, and procedures to make sure there was always a percentage of improvement. A small percentage of improvement each time leads to a greater return in the long term, so do your due diligence. In order to succeed in business, have a robust framework for conducting business.

The best organizations have the following:

- Systems

- Processes

- Efficiencies

- Refining and improving on organization structure with continuous review of roles and responsibilities

What Makes You Money?
Quick Check for Understanding:

_____

_____

_____

Perseverance

So, you've made the decision to get started. Congratulations for simply doing it now! You started. Persevering is important. You will have so many opportunities along the way to quit and to give up, but there are many reasons why you shouldn't. At some point, it may seem that things are not working out the way you planned in your mind. However, I urge you to persevere. Don't give up. Take courage and press on. Keep going. Why did you desire to start this business anyway? Revisit that thought process. Go back through this book and revisit your answers. Also, evaluate your systems and don't get stuck by not continuing to do research and make improvements and adjustments.

Perseverance
Quick Check for Understanding:

_____

_____

_____

Business Growth

When you look at the area of business growth, there are so many myths around selling. Many business owners will say, "Oh, I'm not a salesperson. I don't know how to do it." Personally, I think that's a misguided myth. Everyone sells all the time.

There's a passion naturally coming out of me when I start talking about the things I love to do or the businesses I'm involved in. That in itself is a selling point. You create ambassadors and brand loyalty from the passion and the level of your ability to articulate the service you're providing, so we're selling all the time.

When you walk into a place, a first impression always counts towards what is perceived about what you're about to do or buy. When you look at similar products and must choose one, the look and the appearance of it will determine which one you take. Also, you end up choosing what has been referred by someone else. So, a trusted source gives a testimony about a product, and the solution or passion sells the item. Your friend may say three products are good, so you cut out the other three. You focus on the two based on the trusted referral. We are selling all the time. Create solutions that demonstrate your ability to believe in your own products. Passion sells.

I believe passion sells. If I am convinced that Effie is telling me A or B, she has used it and represents the product well. Therefore, I'm willing to purchase the item, but most people do not consider how they portray themselves. My initial vision for business growth was contained in providing a number of good quality nurses to a number of clients that we would provide services to in a specific geographic region. And the goal was to do that exceptionally well. Also, I wanted to limit the number of locations, so we could control the quality of services provided.

I am a strong believer that anything you put your mind to is possible. I'm actually using a quote from my son. He said, "Oh, I've come to a place where I know that anything that you put your mind to is possible." You can do anything, so I say the same, in terms of starting and growing a business. Anything that you conceive, both success and failure—if you put your mind to it and you really act on it, you'll achieve it, both either the success or the failure.

Here's another quote from my son: "You should not put your shortcomings ahead of your dreams." What he means by this is sometimes we get so consumed in the areas we perceive to be lacking that we deem ourselves to be inadequate to do what we can do, what we are called to do, what we are gifted to do.

I believe that despite our shortcomings, when entrepreneurs dare to diligently apply themselves, the business owner will provide a solution—not only for their own environment, but even a global solution.

Sometimes, all it took was a negative word from a parent, teacher, spouse, or someone within their network of trusted sources or support to put a little doubt in them. To the extent, the doubt became bigger than the dream and the vision they had.

When Myles Munroe said, "The wealthiest place in the world is the graveyard or the cemetery," he further explained that a cemetery is a place where a lot of unfulfilled dreams and ambitions rest because many of the people have now gone on. And their dreams and visions were not fulfilled.

I declare, "Go ahead! Take the steps to become the 7-Figure Business Owner that you're passionate about. Use the tools you've learned to ensure you've done your due diligence to build a viable profitable business. I wish you much success!"

Business Growth
Quick Check for Understanding:

_____

_____

_____

Chapter Seven

ACTION STEPS
Apply What You've Learned

Creating Business Value

Business value comes from...

Evidence of value generating business...

Making Money Work for You

- How do you monetize your plan?

- What are your distribution channels and networks required?

- There's no "one size fits all" for each financial plan. What changes and adjustments do you need to make?

- How many processes can be automated?

Who's On Your Winning Team? Checklist

☐ Finance expert (Accountant/Bookkeeper)

☐ Banker (with services for the long term)

☐ Marketing (understanding the marketplace)

☐ Insurance and business liability

☐ Support network (mentors, leaders in business)

☐ Intellectual capital

☐ YOU—your value as a business owner, your attitude about money

"IT IS IMPORTANT TO HAVE YOUR WINNING TEAM."

7-FIGURE BUSINESS OWNER STRATEGIC PLAN

INSTRUCTIONS: You will create your 7-Figure Business Owner Strategic Plan on the final pages. You have answered many of these questions already. You are simply creating a document of your research and placing the information on the pages provided. Once you are done, follow the directions to create the final electronic presentation.

BUSINESS NAME

BUSINESS OVERVIEW

What products or services does your business provide?

EXECUTIVE SUMMARY

Define the business concept/idea:

What is the gap you will fill?

Snapshot of business viability (financial success):

What is your unique selling proposition?

What is distinctive about your product/services?

INTRODUCTION

Company description:

Business name and location:

What is the history/motivation behind why you started your business?

MISSION, VISION, AND VALUE

Mission:

Vision:

Values:

BUSINESS OBJECTIVES

Why does the business exist and what do you plan to achieve in the:

Short Term?

Medium Term?

Long Term?

IDENTIFY THE PROBLEMS

What is the problem you're going to solve?

What product plan, customer feedback, or insight led to this project?

Why should it happen now?

Compelling presentation of what your business will solve:

Facts and data to support your assumptions:

IDENTIFY THE MARKET

What is your market? What do you understand about your market?

Who are your customers?

What is the specific segment/sector/niche to be serviced?

Who are your competitors?

Who is doing it well already? How are they doing it well?

What is the opportunity or room for improvement that
your business will solve?

If the market is saturated, how will you win customers over to your business?

What innovation/creativity differentiates you from others in your market?

What are the risks, and how do you prepare to succeed with that knowledge?

WHO ARE YOUR COMPETITORS?

Summarize what they do well and what makes them stand out:

**Find a weakness or key they seem to be leaving unattended.
Could this be an opportunity for you?**

VALUE PROPOSITION

What value will you bring?

What is the Return On Investment (ROI) of the solution you've proposed?

How will it improve service delivery and customer experience?

What is distinct about your brand/product/services?

Why is your business relevant?

MARKETING STRATEGY

What is your market? What do you understand about your market?

How might you use traditional media like print, billboards, etc.?

Explain how you might use digital media like ads, Instagram, Facebook, etc.

In the face of everchanging business environments, how will you excel?

How/what is the most effective strategic platform for your business?

MARKETING VISION BOARD

What is your mountaintop experience?

PAINT THE PICTURE SO THAT WHEN YOU SEE IT, YOU RUN WITH IT!

FINANCIAL PROJECTIONS

Define the financial viability (size of market, potential income, profit, margins):

How will you charge or price your products and services?

Sales and revenue forecasting:

The budget baseline for your business plan:

Your projected revenue for the first three years:

Your plan to manage finances:

Legal entities, company formation, licensing requirements, and related implications:

Your current and future business finances:

Access to finances, funding your business, and realizing the vision:

YOUR TEAM

Who is your team (short-term, medium-term, long-term)?

What is the personnel structure that will support your business model?

What support system, external partners, collaborations, and partnerships are planned?

What model of business do you plan to have?

How will your structure be sustainable in a changing business environment?

LEGAL STRUCTURE

What is the business formation structure (type of business, implications for each structure)?

What tax identifications or registrations required? What is essential, and what is mandatory for your industry? What are regulatory requirements? What is mandated and essential?

What license and permits do you need (external accreditations and licensing)?

What protection and business insurance are required?

What regulatory requirements must the business comply to?

What services do you need to get started?
Bookkeeper/HR, external partners, service level agreements, formal work arrangements and rules of engagements

THREE SIMPLE GOALS

1.

2.

3.

NOW CREATE YOUR 7-FIGURE BUSINESS OWNER POWERPOINT OR GOOGLE SLIDE PRESENTATION!

I wish you much success! Remember to review your process daily and weekly with your team to be watchful over your investment! Also, remain close to our professional development group(s) for support. There is always something new to learn or review.

Effie

7-Figure Business Owner, Coach, and Author

WANT TO PROVIDE VALUABLE FEEDBACK AND GET FURTHER SUPPORT?

Scan this code to take the free follow-up assessment:

REFERENCES

Aguilar, F. J. (1967). Scanning the Business Environment (3rd ed.). MacMillan, New York. (PESTEL Analysis)

Silva, Carlos Nunes (2005). "SWOT analysis". In Caves, Roger W. (ed.). Encyclopedia of the city. Abingdon; New York: Routledge. pp. 444–445. doi:10.4324/9780203484234. ISBN 978-0415862875. OCLC 55948158. (SWOT Analysis)

Made in the USA
Columbia, SC
11 November 2024

46057180R00085